COMMON CORE
MATH 5
WORKBOOK

prepaze

www.prepaze.com

Author: Ace Academic Publishing

Ace Academic Publishing is a leading supplemental educational workbook publisher for grades K-12. At Ace Academic Publishing, we realize the importance of imparting analytical and critical thinking skills during the early ages of childhood and hence our books include materials that require multiple levels of analysis and encourage the students to think outside the box.

The materials for our books are written by award winning teachers with several years of teaching experience. All our books are aligned with the state standards and are widely used by many schools throughout the country.

Prepaze is a sister company of Ace Academic Publishing. Intrigued by the unending possibilities of the internet and its role in education, Prepaze was created to spread the knowledge and learning across all corners of the world through an online platform. We equip ourselves with state-of-the-art technologies so that knowledge reaches the students through the quickest and the most effective channels.

For inquiries and bulk orders, contact Ace Academic Publishing at the following address:

Ace Academic Publishing
3736 Fallon Road #403
Dublin CA 94568

www.aceacademicpublishing.com

 Ace Academic Publishing
ACHIEVING EXCELLENCE TOGETHER

ISBN:978-1-949383-29-4

INTRODUCTION

About the Book

The contents of this book includes multiple chapters and units covering all the required Common Core Standards for this grade level. Similar to a standardized exam, you can find questions of all types, including multiple choice, fill-in-the-blank, true or false, matching and free response questions. These carefully written questions aim to help students reason abstractly and quantitatively using various models, strategies, and problem-solving techniques. The detailed answer explanations in the back of the book help the students understand the topics and gain confidence in solving similar problems.

For the Parents

This workbook includes practice questions and tests that cover all the required Common Core Standards for the grade level. The book is comprised of multiple tests for each topic so that your child can have an abundant amount of tests on the same topic. The workbook is divided into chapters and units so that you can choose the topics that you want your child needs to focus on. The detailed answer explanations in the back will teach your child the right methods to solve the problems for all types of questions, including the free-response questions. After completing the tests on all the chapters, your child can take any Common Core standardized exam with confidence and can excel in it.

For additional online practice, sign up for a free account at www.aceacademicprep.com.

For the Teachers

All questions and tests included in this workbook are based on the Common Core State Standards and includes a clear label of each standard name. You can assign your students tests on a particular unit in each chapter, and can also assign a chapter review test. The book also includes two final exams which you can use towards the end of the school year to review all the topics that were covered. This workbook will help your students overcome any deficiencies in their understanding of critical concepts and will also help you identify the specific topics that your students may require additional practice. These grade-appropriate, yet challenging, questions will help your students learn to strategically use appropriate tools and excel in Common Core standardized exams.

For additional online practice, sign up for a free account at www.aceacademicprep.com.

www.prepaze.com

Other books from Ace Academic Publishing

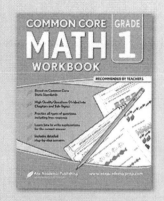   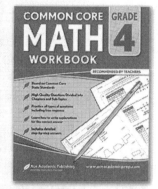

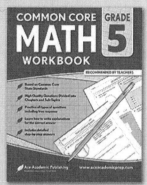  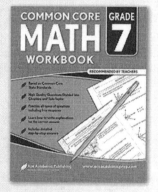 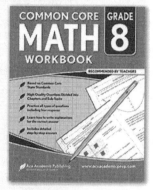

  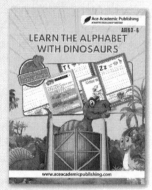 

TABLE OF CONTENTS

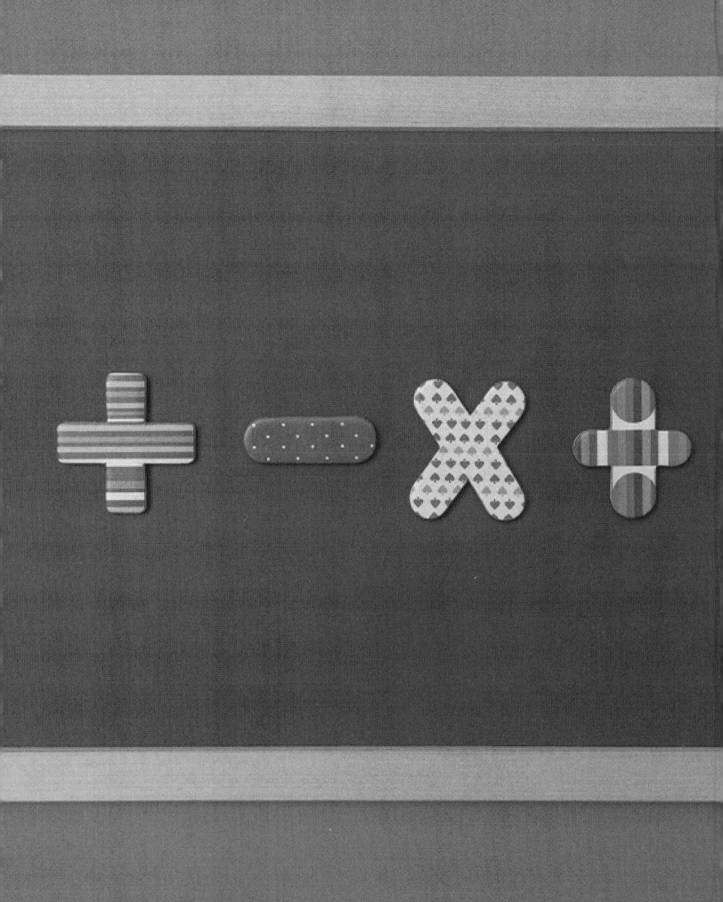

OPERATIONS & ALGEBRAIC THINKING

prepaze

www.prepaze.com

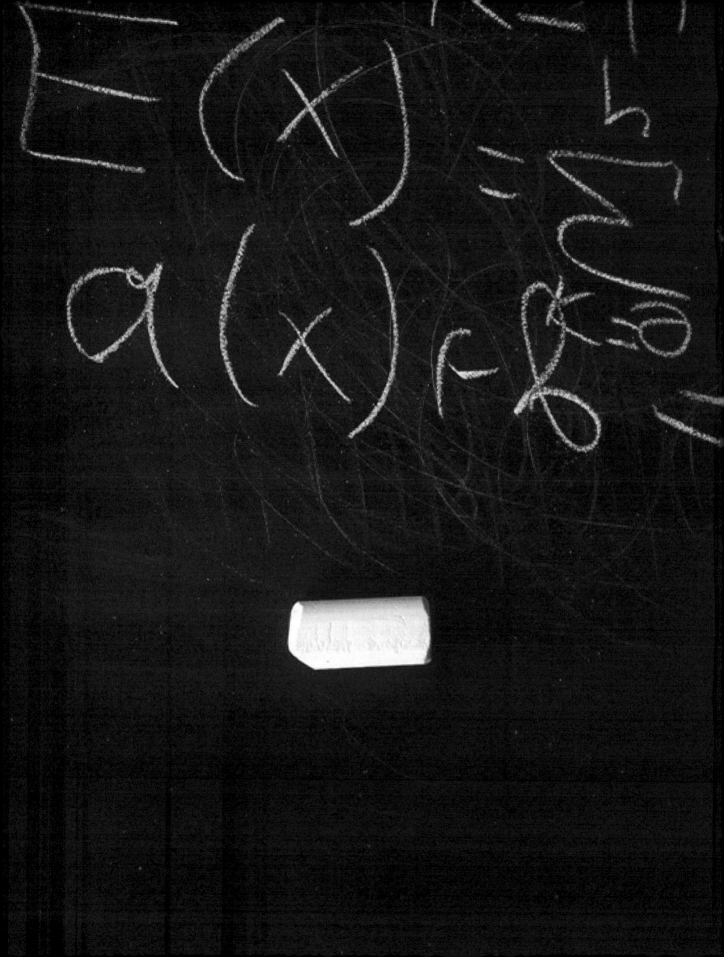

OPERATIONS & ALGEBRAIC THINKING

1. Jessica is simplifying this expression: $100 \div [5 \times (16 - 6)]$. She believes she should multiply 5 and 16 first. Do you agree or disagree? Why?

_____

_____

_____

5.OA.A.1

2. Maria is simplifying this expression $6 - 14 + 9 \times 5$. What should she do first? Explain your reasoning.

_____

_____

_____

5.OA.A.1

3. Scott is simplifying this expression.

$$9 + 72 \times 2$$

He says that he is going to add 9 and 72 first. What do you tell him?

_____

_____

_____

5.OA.A.1

prepaze

OPERATIONS & ALGEBRAIC THINKING

4. Jacob is solving the problem $17 \times 3 + (5 + 11)$. What should he do first? Explain your thinking.

_____

_____

_____

5.OA.A.1

5. Which expression has a value of 15?

A. $(5 + 3) \div 1$

B. $5 \times (3 + 2)$

C. $5 \times (3 \times 1)$

D. $5 - 3 \times 1$

5.OA.A.1

6. What is the value of this expression? $(5 + 20) \div 5$

A. 9

B. 5

C. 25

D. 10

5.OA.A.1

7. Simplify:
$15 + [6 \times (9 + 1)]$.

A. 75

B. 54

C. 70

D. 80

5.OA.A.1

8. Which expression has a value of 17?

A. $30 - (3 - 1) \div 2$

B. $2 + (3 \times 5)$

C. $5 \times (6 \div 2)$

D. $(5 - 3) \times 2$

5.OA.A.1

9. Which expression has a value of 75?

A. $(15 \times 8) - 3$

B. $(15 \times 8 - 3)$

C. $15 \times (8 - 3)$

D. $15 \times 8 - 3$

5.OA.A.1

OPERATIONS & ALGEBRAIC THINKING

10. Udella writes an expression that has a value of 50. Where should she place the parentheses to make this expression have a value of 50?

$$10 \times 10 \div 16 - 14$$

A. Around 10 times 10

B. Around 10 divided by 16

C. Around 16 minus 14

D. Around 10 divided by 16 minus 14

5.OA.A.1

WRITE NUMERICAL EXPRESSIONS

11. Which expression follows this story?

"I have 11 boxes of crayons. Each box of crayons has 6 crayons in the first row and 6 crayons in the second row."

A. $11 \times 6 + 6$

B. $(11 \times 6) \times 6$

C. $(11 \times 6) + 6$

D. $11 \times (6 + 6)$

5.OA.A.1

12. Edward writes an expression that has a value of 18. Which expression has the parentheses and bracket in the correct place?

A. $2 \times [81 \div (4 + 5)]$

B. $2 \times [81 \div 4 + 5]$

C. $[2 \times (81 \div 4 + 5)]$

D. $2 \times 81 \div 4 + 5$

5.OA.A.1

13. Which symbol should be used to compare the two expressions?

$$14 + [24 \div (8 + 4)] \underline{\hspace{3cm}} 6 + (3 \times 11) - 8$$

A. >   **B.** <   **C.** =   **D.** Not enough information.

5.OA.A.1

prepaze

OPERATIONS & ALGEBRAIC THINKING

WRITE NUMERICAL EXPRESSIONS

14. This expression is equivalent to 15. What is the value of *x*?

$$x \div (29 - 24) - 15$$

A. 75 **B.** 68 **C.** 185 **D.** 150

5.OA.A.1

15. This expression has a value of 60. What is the value of *c*?

$$c(27 - 17)$$

A. 9 **B.** 7 **C.** 6 **D.** 8

5.OA.A.1

16. What is the value of this expression?

$$100 - [(4 + 18) \times 2]$$

A. 75 **B.** 56 **C.** 85 **D.** 80

5.OA.A.1

17. Which symbol should be used to compare the two expressions?

$$50 - [2 \times (4 + 4)] \underline{\hspace{2cm}} 17 + (39 \div 3) + 8$$

A. > **B.** < **C.** = **D.** Not enough information.

5.OA.A.1

18. What is the value of this expression?

$$4 \times [(14 + 17) - (5 + 3)]$$

A. 84 **B.** 101 **C.** 92 **D.** 98

5.OA.A.1

OPERATIONS & ALGEBRAIC THINKING

19. Which symbol should be used to compare the two expressions?

$$4 \times [9 \div (2+1)] \underline{\hspace{2cm}} 60 - [(9 \times 3)+8]$$

A. > **B.** < **C.** = **D.** Not enough information.

5.OA.A.1

20. This expression has a value of 120. What is the value of **m**?

$$m + 4 \times 10$$

A. 8 **B.** 7 **C.** 60 **D.** 80

5.OA.A.1

UNIT 2:   INTERPRET NUMERICAL EXPRESSIONS

prepaze

OPERATIONS & ALGEBRAIC THINKING

INTERPRET NUMERICAL EXPRESSIONS

1. How can this expression be written in words?

$$(54 + 132) \times 4$$

_____

_____

_____

5.OA.A.2

2. How can this expression be written in words?

$$5 \times (3 + 2)$$

_____

_____

_____

5.OA.A.2

3. Your friend is writing an expression for twice as much as the difference between 587 and 453. He wrote $(587 - 453) \div 2$. Do you agree or disagree? Why?

_____

_____

_____

5.OA.A.2

OPERATIONS & ALGEBRAIC THINKING

4. Does the expression $3 \times 675 + 93$ show three times the sum of six hundred seventy-five and ninety-three? Why or why not?

_____

_____

_____

5.OA.A.2

5. The expression $12 \times (17 + 152)$ means:

A. The product of 12, 17 and 152.

B. The product of 12 and 152 added to 17.

C. The product of 12 and the difference of 152 and 17.

D. The product of 12 and the sum of 17 and 152.

5.OA.A.2

6. The expression $4 \times (5184 + 171)$ means:

A. Four times 5,184 and 171.

B. Four times more than 5,184 minus 171.

C. Four more than 5,184 and 171.

D. Four times the sum of 5,184 and 171.

5.OA.A.2

7. Which expression matches this description?

Add 17 and 4, then multiply the sum by 3.

A. $17 + 4 \times 3$ **B.** $(17 + 4) \times 3$

C. $17 + (4 \times 3)$ **D.** $(17 + 4 \times 3)$

5.OA.A.2

INTERPRET NUMERICAL EXPRESSIONS

prepaze

OPERATIONS & ALGEBRAIC THINKING

8. The expression $3 \times (15 + 4)$ can be written as:

  A. Three times the sum of 15 and 4

  B. Three times 4 plus 15

  C. Three times more than the sum of 15 and 4

  D. Three times more than the difference between 15 and 4

(5.OA.A.2)

9. Theresa writes an expression that means "The quotient of 862 and 2 subtracted from 2,651". Which symbol is missing from the expression?

$$2,651 - 862 \underline{\quad} 2$$

  A. $\div$ **B.** $\times$ **C.** $+$ **D.** $-$

(5.OA.A.2)

10. Which numerical expression represents this verbal expression?

Multiply 16 and 3, then add the difference of 7 and 1.

  A. $(16 \times 3) + (7 - 1)$ **B.** $16 \times (3 + 7) + 1$

  C. $16 \times (3 + 7 - 1)$ **D.** $16 \times 3 \times 7 + 1$

(5.OA.A.2)

11. Which statement describes this expression?

$$(3,989 + 67) \times 4$$

  A. 67 more than 3,839

  B. A quantity 4 times larger than 3,839

  C. A quantity 4 times the sum of 3,839 and 67

  D. 3,839 more than 4 times 67

(5.OA.A.2)

OPERATIONS & ALGEBRAIC THINKING

12. Which statement describes this expression?

$$(100 - 15) \times 3$$

A. Fifteen less than 100, tripled

B. Fifteen more than 100, tripled

C. Three times 100 plus 15

D. Three times 15 minus 100

5.OA.A.2

13. Write an expression that shows 40 divided by the sum of 4 and 1.

_____

5.OA.A.2

14. The expression $9 \times (3 + 7)$ means nine _____ the sum of three and seven.

5.OA.A.2

15. What symbol is needed to create this expression?

8 times the product of 43 and 961

$8 \times (43 \underline{\hphantom{xx}} 961)$

5.OA.A.2

16. Write an expression to represent the product of 11 and 6 increased by 7.

_____

5.OA.A.2

prepaze

OPERATIONS & ALGEBRAIC THINKING

17. **True or False:** 14 times the sum of 16 and 765 can be written as $14 \times 16 + 765$.

_____

5.OA.A.2

18. **True or False:** The expression $(2371 - 17) \div 2$ means the difference of 2,371 and 17 divided by 2.

_____

5.OA.A.2

19. **True or False:** The numerical expression that represents 17 times the sum of 975 and 72 is $17 \times (975 \times 72)$.

_____

5.OA.A.2

20. **True or False:** The expression $5 \times (685 + 127)$ means 5 times the sum of 685 and 127.

_____

5.OA.A.2

UNIT 3:   **WRITE NUMERICAL EXPRESSIONS PATTERNS**

OPERATIONS & ALGEBRAIC THINKING

1. John is describing the rule used to create a graph. Each x-value has a rule to "add 2". Each y-value has a rule to "add 4". If the first ordered pair in the sequence is (2, 4), what is the second ordered pair. How do you know?

_____

_____

_____

5.OA.B.3

2. What are the two rules of this function table? How do you know?

x	6	12	18
y	9	6	3

_____

_____

_____

5.OA.B.3

3. Lara is describing the rule used to create a graph. Each x-value has a rule to "add 3". Each y-value has a rule to "subtract 1". If the first ordered pair in the sequence is (1, 10), what is the second ordered pair in the sequence? How do you know?

_____

_____

_____

5.OA.B.3

prepaze

OPERATIONS & ALGEBRAIC THINKING

4. What pattern do you notice in this function table? Explain your thinking.

x	3	4	5
y	6	8	10

_____

_____

_____

5.OA.B.3

5. The rules for this pattern are $x = +4$, $y = +2$.

Where will the next point be placed on the graph?

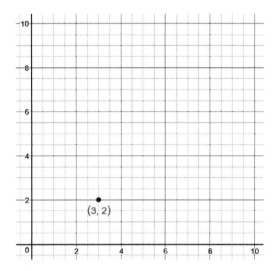

(3, 2)

A. (3, 2)

B. (7, 4)

C. (5, 6)

D. (6, 5)

5.OA.B.3

6. Which ordered pair is missing in this function table?

x	1	4	?	10
y	10	8	?	4

A. (6, 8)   **B.** (7, 6)

C. (7, 8)   **D.** (6, 7)

5.OA.B.3

OPERATIONS & ALGEBRAIC THINKING

7. What number is missing from this table?

x	2	4	6
y	6	8	?

A. 6
B. 9
C. 10
D. 12

5.OA.B.3

8. The rules for this pattern are $x = -2, y = +1$.

What other ordered pair matches this pattern?

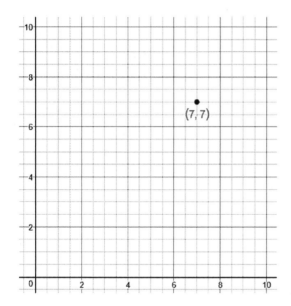

(7, 7)

A. (7, 7)

B. (9, 8)

C. (5, 8)

D. (9, 6)

5.OA.B.3

9. Three ordered pairs in a sequence are (6, 5), (12, 10), (18, 15).
What is the rule for finding the next y-value?

A. Add 5
C. Multiply by 3

B. Multiply by 2
D. Add 6

5.OA.B.3

prepaze

OPERATIONS & ALGEBRAIC THINKING

WRITE NUMERICAL EXPRESSIONS PATTERNS

10. Which number is missing in the function table?

x	15	14	13	12
y	15	13	?	9

A. 9　　　　　　**B.** 10

C. 11　　　　　**D.** 12

(5.OA.B.3)

11. Three ordered pairs in a sequence are (12, 3), (9, 5), (6, 7). What is the rule for finding the next x-value?

A. Add three　　　　　　**B.** Add two

C. Subtract three　　　　　**D.** Subtract two

(5.OA.B.3)

12. Three ordered pairs in a sequence are (3, 7), (6, 14), (9, 21). What would the ordered pair just before (3, 7) be?

A. (1, 1)　　　**B.** (12, 29)　　　**C.** (6, 14)　　　**D.** (0, 0)

(5.OA.B.3)

13. What number is missing from the table?

x	34	26	18	10
y	26	18	?	2

A. 8　　　　　　**B.** 10

C. 14　　　　　**D.** 12

(5.OA.B.3)

14. Which ordered pair is missing in the function table?

x	4	6	8	?
y	5	10	15	?

A. (10, 18)　　　**B.** (10, 20)

C. (12, 20)　　　**D.** (12, 10)

(5.OA.B.3)

OPERATIONS & ALGEBRAIC THINKING

15. In the function table, how much greater is each y-value compared to each x-value?

x	1	2	3	4
y	10	11	12	13

A. 8   **B.** 6

C. 10   **D.** 9

(5.OA.B.3)

16. The rule of a function is "each y-value is 3 times each x-value". What is the value of x when y is 6?

A. 2   **B.** 3   **C.** 5   **D.** 2.5

(5.OA.B.3)

17. True or False: The rule of the table is $y = x + 11$.

x	5	7	9
y	17	19	21

_____

(5.OA.B.3)

18. True or False: Jessica is starting at (0, 0) and creating a graph according to this rule: "add 5 to each x-value and add 3 to each y-value".

The second ordered pair in this sequence will be (3, 5).

_____

(5.OA.B.3)

prepaze

OPERATIONS & ALGEBRAIC THINKING

19. Joshua plots a point on the graph at (7,7). He wants to plot another point according to this rule:

x-**value:** multiply by 2

y-**value:** divide by 7

Write an ordered pair to represent a point on Joshua's graph.

_____

5.OA.B.3

20. True or False: A rule for this table could be $x = y - 5$.

x	14	13	12
y	19	18	17

_____

5.OA.B.3

prepaze

OPERATIONS & ALGEBRAIC THINKING

1. Marcus is simplifying this expression: $4 + (6 + 28) \div 2$.

He believes that he needs to add 6 and 28 as a first step. Do you agree or disagree? Explain your reasoning.

_____

_____

_____

5.OA.A.1

2. Your sister sees the parentheses in a numerical expression you are simplifying. She asks what they mean. What do you tell her?

_____

_____

_____

5.OA.A.1

3. There are 6 tables in a classroom with 15 pencils and 6 pens on each table. Write an expression to represent the number of pencils and pens in the classroom. Explain your reasoning.

_____

_____

_____

5.OA.A.1

prepaze

OPERATIONS & ALGEBRAIC THINKING

CHAPTER REVIEW

4. My friend has 85 pennies and last week I had 5 times fewer pennies. This week I found 29 pennies. Write an expression to represent the number of pennies I have now. Explain your reasoning.

_____

_____

_____

5.OA.A.1

5. This expression has a value of 72. What is the value of **x**?

$$4(35 - x) + 4$$

A. 12   **B.** 15   **C.** 18   **D.** 14

5.OA.A.1

6. Which symbol should be used to compare the two expressions?

$$2 \times [9 \times (2 + 1)] \rule{2cm}{0.4pt} 50 \div [(2 \times 3) + 4]$$

A. >   **B.** <   **C.** =   **D.** Not enough information.

5.OA.A.1

7. This expression has a value of 45. What is the value of **n**?

$$5 + (n \times 10)$$

A. 6   **B.** 5   **C.** 4   **D.** 2

5.OA.A.1

OPERATIONS & ALGEBRAIC THINKING

8. Write a numerical expression to represent this verbal expression:

Multiply the sum of 8 and 17 by 4

Explain your reasoning.

_____

_____

_____

5.OA.A.2

9. How can the expression $(654 - 14) \div 2$ be written in words?

_____

_____

_____

5.OA.A.2

10. How can this expression be represented numerically?

The product of 5 and 8 decreased by 4.

Explain your thinking.

_____

_____

_____

5.OA.A.2

prepaze

OPERATIONS & ALGEBRAIC THINKING

11. Does the expression $(5765 - 135) \div 2$ show half of the difference between 5765 and 135? Explain your reasoning.

_____

_____

_____

5.OA.A.2

12. Add the missing symbol to create an expression that represents 8 times less than the sum of 72 and 64.

$$(72 \_\_\_\_ 64) \div 8$$

5.OA.A.2

13. Write a numerical expression that shows 10 times the difference of 15 and 9.

_____

5.OA.A.2

14. James is graphing the ordered pairs for the rule $y = x + 2$. He plots the first point at (2,4). Where could the next 3 points be placed? Explain your reasoning.

_____

_____

_____

5.OA.B.3

OPERATIONS & ALGEBRAIC THINKING

15. Samantha is graphing the ordered pairs for a sequence that starts at (2, 7). She will continue the sequence using this rule: $y = 5 + x$. Write one ordered pair which could belong in this sequence.

_____

5.OA.B.3

16. What is the rule for the pattern shown in this table? Explain your thinking.

x	8	10	12
y	14	16	18

_____

_____

_____

5.OA.B.3

17. What number is missing in the pattern? How do you know?

x	3	10	17	24
y	10	17	24	?

_____

_____

_____

5.OA.B.3

18. The rule for the table is $y = x + 11$. What is the missing number?

x	1	2	3
y	?	13	14

A. 11   **B.** 12
C. 15   **D.** 10

5.OA.B.3

prepaze

OPERATIONS & ALGEBRAIC THINKING

19. The first ordered pair in a sequence is (2, 4). The rules for the sequence are $x = +3$ and $y = +5$. What will the third ordered pair in the sequence be?

A. (5, 9) **B.** (8, 14) **C.** (7, 14) **D.** (6, 17)

(5.OA.B.3)

20. The rule of a function is the y-value is 13 more than each x-value. What is the value of x when y is 25?

A. 15 **B.** 11 **C.** 14 **D.** 12

(5.OA.B.3)

EXTRA PRACTICE

OPERATIONS & ALGEBRAIC THINKING

1. Jermia is simplifying this expression:

$$[100 - (64 + 15)] \times (38 - 22)$$

Which response shows how this expression can be rewritten?

A. $(100 - 64) + (15 \times 38) - 22$

B. $(100 - 64 - 15) \times (38 - 22)$

C. $100 - (64 + 15 \times 38) - 22$

D. $100 - (64 + 15 \times 38 - 22)$

5.OA.A.1

2. What part of this expression should be evaluated first?

$$7 + \{14 \times [8 + (10 \times 3)]\}$$

A. $7 + 14$ **B.** $8 + 10$ **C.** 10×3 **D.** 14×8

5.OA.A.1

3. A square has side lengths that are $(3 + 4) + 7$ units long. What is the perimeter of this square?

_____

5.OA.A.1

4. John walks every other week for 3 years. He walks 3 miles every week that he walks. There are 52 weeks in one year. Write two expressions to represent the total number of miles John walks.

_____

5.OA.A.1

prepaze

OPERATIONS & ALGEBRAIC THINKING

5. What is the value of this expression?

$$25 + [(12 \times 10) + 4 \times (15 - 7)]$$

_____

5.OA.A.1

6. Lana believes these expressions have the same value:

$$[(32 - 19) - 15 - 2] \qquad [32 - 19 - (15 - 2)]$$

Do you agree with Lana? Explain your reasoning.

_____

_____

_____

5.OA.A.1

7. What is the value of this expression?

$$38 + 56 \div (4 \times 2) - 3$$

_____

5.OA.A.1

8. Whitney writes these two expressions:

Expression A: _____ $\times (4 + 7) \times 8$

Expression B: $(4 + 7) \times 8 \times 4$

Expression A is 3 times greater than Expression B. What is the missing value?

A. 3   **B.** 7   **C.** 4   **D.** 12

5.OA.A.2

OPERATIONS & ALGEBRAIC THINKING

9. Which phrase represents this expression?

$$9 - 4(10 + 7)$$

A. The difference between 9 and 4 times the sum of 10 and 7

B. The difference of 9 and 4, multiplied by the product of 10 and 7

C. The quotient of 9 and 4, added to the product of 10 and 7

D. The quotient of 9 and 4, added to the sum of 10 and 7

(5.OA.A.2)

10. Write an expression to represent four times the sum of fifty-four and six divided, all divided by eight minus two.

_____

(5.OA.A.2)

11. Write an expression to represent this calculation:

Add 14 and 8, then multiply by the product of 5 and 3.

_____

(5.OA.A.2)

12. Write an expression to represent this calculation:

Twice the quotient of 45 and 9, then divided by 5.

_____

(5.OA.A.2)

prepaze

OPERATIONS & ALGEBRAIC THINKING

13. Hunter translates "five times the sum of one hundred three thousand, six hundred eight and forty-three thousand, twenty-one" as this numerical expression:

$$5(100,368 + 43,021)$$

Do you agree with Hunter?

_____

_____

_____

_____

(5.OA.A.2)

14. Reynaldo translates "the product of eighteen and nineteen divided by the product of three and zero" as this numerical expression:

$$\frac{(18 \times 19)}{(3 \times 0)}$$

Do you agree with Reynaldo?

_____

_____

_____

_____

(5.OA.A.2)

OPERATIONS & ALGEBRAIC THINKING

15. Which ordered pair is missing from this table?

x	y
2	17
6	14
14	8

A. (4, 3) **B.** (6, 11)

C. (10, 11) **D.** (18, 15)

5.OA.B.3

16. Which ordered pair is missing from this table?

x	y
19	7
14	10
9	13

A. (24, 4) **B.** (14, 4)

C. (24, 10) **D.** (14, 17)

5.OA.B.3

17. What two rules are used to create this table?

x	y
12	11
21	9
30	7
39	5

x-values: _____

y-values: _____

5.OA.B.3

18. What two rules are used to create this table?

x	y
8	1,000
24	200
72	40
216	8

x-values: _____

y-values: _____

5.OA.B.3

prepaze

OPERATIONS & ALGEBRAIC THINKING

19. What rule can be used to describe the points on this graph?

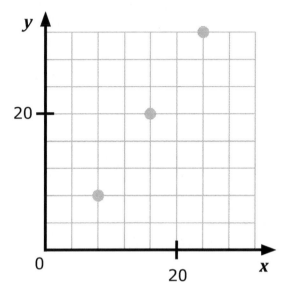

x-values: _____

y-values: _____

5.OA.B.3

20. What rule can be used to describe the points on this graph?

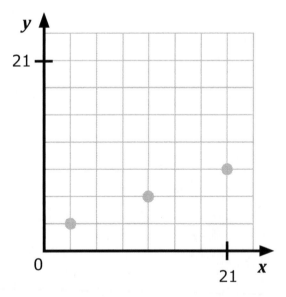

x-values: _____

y-values: _____

5.OA.B.3

NUMBER & OPERATIONS IN BASE TEN

prepaze

www.prepaze.com

NUMBER & OPERATIONS IN BASE TEN

1. Evaluate: $5,000 \div 500 =$ _____

    A. 50   **B.** 10

    C. 5   **D.** 500

5.NBT.A.1

2. Evaluate: $67.54 \div 10 =$ _____

    A. 6754   **B.** 675.4

    C. 6.754   **D.** 0.6754

5.NBT.A.1

3. Evaluate: $9.32 \div 10 =$ _____

    A. 932   **B.** 93.2

    C. 0.932   **D.** 0.0932

5.NBT.A.1

4. Evaluate $7,000 \times \left(\frac{1}{10}\right) =$ _____

    A. 700   **B.** 70

    C. 7   **D.** 0.7

5.NBT.A.1

5. Evaluate $19.8 \times \left(\frac{1}{100}\right) =$ _____

    A. 198   **B.** 1.98

    C. 0.198   **D.** 0.0198

5.NBT.A.1

6. Evaluate $2.65 \times \left(\frac{1}{10}\right) =$ _____

    A. 265   **B.** 26.5

    C. 0.265   **D.** 0.0265

5.NBT.A.1

7. **True or False:** The number 55.5 is 10 times larger than 5.55.

    A. True   **B.** False

5.NBT.A.1

8. **True or False:** The number 34.5 is 100 times larger than 3.45.

    A. True   **B.** False

5.NBT.A.1

9. **True or False:** The number 0.9 is 10 times smaller than 9.

    A. True   **B.** False

5.NBT.A.1

10. **True or False:** The number 6.74 is 100 times smaller than 674.

    A. True   **B.** False

5.NBT.A.1

prepaze

NUMBER & OPERATIONS IN BASE TEN

11. Explain patterns in the number of zeros of the product: 4×10^1.

Place Value Chart						
Millions	Hundred Thousands	Ten Thousands	Thousands	Hundreds	Tens	Ones
10^6	10^5	10^4	10^3	10^2	10^1	10^0

_____

_____

_____

(5.NBT.A.2)

12. Explain patterns in the number of zeros of the product: 7×10^6.

Place Value Chart						
Millions	Hundred Thousands	Ten Thousands	Thousands	Hundreds	Tens	Ones
10^6	10^5	10^4	10^3	10^2	10^1	10^0

_____

_____

_____

(5.NBT.A.2)

13. Evaluate: $538 \times 10^4 =$ _____

A. 5,380   **B.** 53,800   **C.** 538,000   **D.** 5,380,000

(5.NBT.A.2)

NUMBER & OPERATIONS IN BASE TEN

14. Evaluate: $44 \times 10^6 =$ _____

A. 44,000,000

B. 4,400,000

C. 440,000

D. 44,000

(5.NBT.A.2)

15. Evaluate: $899 \times 10^0 =$ _____

A. 899

B. 8,990

C. 89,900

D. 899,000

(5.NBT.A.2)

16. Evaluate: $9.6 \times 10^4 =$ _____

A. 96

B. 960

C. 9,600

D. 96,000

(5.NBT.A.2)

17. There are 10,000 ants living in a colony underground. If that amount doubles in the next year, there will be 20,000 ants living underground. Which equation below is correct?

A. $2 \times 10^1 = 20,000$

B. $2 \times 10^2 = 20,000$

C. $2 \times 10^3 = 20,000$

D. $2 \times 10^4 = 20,000$

(5.NBT.A.2)

18. There is 660,430 gallons of water in an Olympic size swimming pool. Which expression below correctly matches the amount of water in an Olympic size swimming pool?

A. 660.43×10^3 gallons

B. 660.43×10^2 gallons

C. $6,604.3 \times 10^4$ gallons

D. $6,604.3 \times 10^3$ gallons

(5.NBT.A.2)

prepaze

NUMBER & OPERATIONS IN BASE TEN

PLACE VALUE, ROUNDING AND COMPARING

19. True or False: The equivalent form of 8,260 is 82.6×10^4.

    A. True   **B.** False

5.NBT.A.2

20. True or False: The equivalent form of 6.711 is $67.11 \div 10^2$.

    A. True   **B.** False

5.NBT.A.2

UNIT 2: DECIMALS AND DECIMAL OPERATIONS

NUMBER & OPERATIONS IN BASE TEN

1. Write the decimal using base-ten numerals.

Three hundred fifteen and one hundred sixty-two thousandths

_____

5.NBT.A.3

2. Write the decimal using base-ten numerals.

Forty-nine and six hundred eleven thousandths

_____

5.NBT.A.3

3. Write the decimal form of the expression below using base-ten numbers.

$$(3 \times 100) + (4 \times 10) + (7 \times 1) + (3 \times (1/10)) + (9 \times (1/100)) + (2 \times (1/1,000))$$

_____

5.NBT.A.3

4. Compare the two decimals by filling in the box using the >, <, or = symbol.

10.022		10.202

5.NBT.A.3

5. Compare the two decimals by filling in the box using the >, <, or = symbol.

0.050		0.0050

5.NBT.A.3

prepaze

NUMBER & OPERATIONS IN BASE TEN

6. Compare the two decimals by filling in the box using the >, <, or = symbol.

29.816		twenty-nine and eight hundred sixteen thousandths

5.NBT.A.3

7. Compare the two decimals by filling in the box using the >, <, or = symbol.

$(1 \times 100) + (5 \times 10) + (2 \times 1) + (6 \times (1/10))$ $+ (3 \times (1/100)) + (2 \times (1/1,000))$		152.326

5.NBT.A.3

8. When rounding to the nearest hundredth, what place should you review?

A. Tenths
B. Hundredths
C. Thousandths
D. Ten-thousandths

5.NBT.A.4

9. What is the result of rounding 4.9878 to the nearest tenth?

A. 4.9
B. 5.0
C. 4.98
D. 5.1

5.NBT.A.4

10. What is 1794.23836827, rounded to the nearest ten-thousandth?

A. 1794.2383   **B.** 1794.23837

C. 1794.238   **D.** 1794.2384

5.NBT.A.4

NUMBER & OPERATIONS IN BASE TEN

11. Alicia rounded a number to 874.2379 on her math test. To what place was she asked to round?

A. Ten-thousandth   **B.** Thousandth
C. Hundred-thousandth   **D.** Hundredth

5.NBT.A.4

12. John finished the race in 3.6782 minutes. What is his finish time, rounded to the nearest hundredth?

A. 3.678   **B.** 3.689   **C.** 3.67   **D.** 3.68

5.NBT.A.4

13. Mortimer's pet tarantula traveled 3.198 meters in one day. What is this distance, rounded to the nearest hundredth?

A. 3.10   **B.** 3.20   **C.** 3.19   **D.** 3.198

5.NBT.A.4

14. Which response is the best estimate of this expression?

$$84.67 + 29.93$$

A. 100   **B.** 115   **C.** 130   **D.** 55

5.NBT.B.7

15. If Elias's family gave the cashier $40 for a breakfast that cost $29.75, how much change did they receive?

A. $19.25   **B.** $11.75   **C.** $10.25   **D.** $10.75

5.NBT.B.7

DECIMALS AND DECIMAL OPERATIONS

NUMBER & OPERATIONS IN BASE TEN

DECIMALS AND DECIMAL OPERATIONS

16. What is the value of n if $n \times 0.8 = 6.4$?

    A. 80   **B.** 0.08   **C.** 0.8   **D.** 8

5.NBT.B.7

17. Justin went to school for 23 days in September. If he paid $2.90 for lunch each day, about how much did he pay for lunch in September?

    A. $69   **B.** $40   **C.** $90   **D.** $25

5.NBT.B.7

18. Which factor when multiplied by 4.25 gives you a product of 34?

    A. 8   **B.** 9   **C.** 7   **D.** 7.5

5.NBT.B.7

19. Eleanor bought a toy that cost $46.21. If she paid the cashier $52.76 at the register, how much was the sales tax?

_____

5.NBT.B.7

20. What is the value of y if $9 \times y = 4.5$?

_____

5.NBT.B.7

UNIT 3: MULTIPLY AND DIVIDE

NUMBER & OPERATIONS IN BASE TEN

1. Given the dividend of 64 and the quotient of 2, what is the divisor?

A. 26   **B.** 28

C. 30   **D.** 32

5.NBT.B.6

2. Given the dividend of 72 and the divisor of 4, what is the quotient?

A. 14   **B.** 16

C. 18   **D.** 20

5.NBT.B.6

3. If the divisor is 6, and the quotient is 8, what is the dividend?

A. 46   **B.** 48

C. 50   **D.** 52

5.NBT.B.6

4. What is the best expression to use to estimate $6,629 \div 3 = ?$

A. $6600 \div 3$ **B.** $6000 \div 3$

C. $6500 \div 3$ **D.** $7000 \div 3$

5.NBT.B.6

5. Alicia rode her bike for 4 hours and went 60 miles. About how far did she bike per hour?

A. 15 miles

B. 17 miles

C. 240 miles

D. 56 miles

5.NBT.B.6

6. A runner ran 212 miles in 6 days to prepare for a marathon. About how many miles did he run per day?

A. 30 miles

B. 40 miles

C. 35 miles

D. 45 miles

5.NBT.B.6

prepaze

NUMBER & OPERATIONS IN BASE TEN

MULTIPLY AND DIVIDE

7. Given a dividend of 960 and the quotient of 10, what is the divisor?

_____

5.NBT.B.6

8. If the dividend is 128 and the divisor is 4, what is the quotient?

_____

5.NBT.B.6

9. Given a divisor of 20 and a quotient of 14, what is the dividend?

_____

5.NBT.B.6

10. A charity collected $37,000, in equal amounts, from 600 donors. About how much money did each donor give?

A. $600   **B.** $6000   **C.** $6   **D.** $70   **E.** $60

5.NBT.B.6

11. There are multiple questions on a gameshow. There are five 500-point questions and four 400-point questions. How many points are there in each episode?

A. 3100 points   **B.** 4100 points   **C.** 2500 points   **D.** 1600 points

5.NBT.B.5

NUMBER & OPERATIONS IN BASE TEN

12. Maria earns $12 for every hour she works. If she works 8 hours a day, four days a week, how much does she earn in a week?

A. $96   **B.** $400   **C.** $24   **D.** $384

5.NBT.B.5

13. Triplets have the same birthday. Each child invited 8 friends to their birthday party. Each friend brought 2 presents. How many presents were there at the party?

A. 30 presents
B. 13 presents
C. 48 presents
D. 64 presents

5.NBT.B.5

14. The fifth-grade class went to the movies. If 320 students and 15 teachers went and each ticket costs $8, how much money did they spend?

A. $2,680
B. $2,560
C. $2,440
D. $2,800

5.NBT.B.5

15. Each child in a class has a box of 18 crayons. If there are 22 children in the class, how many crayons are there?

A. 40 crayons   **B.** 4 crayons   **C.** 400 crayons   **D.** 396 crayons

5.NBT.B.5

16. What is the product of the three numbers 128, 829 and 4?

A. 320,485   **B.** 212,352   **C.** 424,448   **D.** 106,112

5.NBT.B.5

17. A delivery truck is driven 50 miles per hour. It is driven 9 hours each day. How many miles will it have traveled in 2 days?

A. 450 miles   **B.** 900 miles   **C.** 61 miles   **D.** 1350 miles

5.NBT.B.5

NUMBER & OPERATIONS IN BASE TEN

MULTIPLY AND DIVIDE

18. What is the product of 9, 64, and 28?

_____

5.NBT.B.5

19. Conner mows a lawn in his neighborhood in about 3 hours. How long will it take him to mow 18 lawns of the same size?

_____

5.NBT.B.5

20. Students from 8 fifth grade classrooms wrote letters to their local representatives supporting their school. If each class had 22 students and each student wrote letters to 4 representatives, how many letters did they write?

_____

5.NBT.B.5

CHAPTER REVIEW

NUMBER & OPERATIONS IN BASE TEN

1. Brittney has 1,180.9 yards of ribbon. She wants to cut the ribbon into 10 equal pieces. How long will each piece of ribbon be?

   A. 118.09 yards   **B.** 11.809 yards
   C. 1.1809 yards   **D.** 0.11809 yards

   (5.NBT.A.1)

2. The teacher bought 37.3 ounces of juice for a party. The teacher spilled 2.7 ounces of the juice on the floor. If each of the 10 students recieved an equal amount of the remaining juice, how many ounces did each student get?

   A. 3.73 ounces   **B.** 3.46 ounces   **C.** 3.27 ounces   **D.** 0.373 ounces

   (5.NBT.A.1)

3. Mount Everest is 29,029 feet tall. If Jack climbs 1/10 of the way up the mountain, how many feet does he climb?

   A. 2,902.9 feet   **B.** 290.29 feet   **C.** 29.029 feet   **D.** 2.9029 feet

   (5.NBT.A.1)

4. The fifth-grade class took a field trip to the zoo. Admission cost $14.75 per student. What is the total admission cost for 100 students? Include units.

   _____

   (5.NBT.A.2)

5. A concert hall has 10,000 seats, and tickets cost $120.50 per seat. What is the total ticket sales if the concert hall is sold out?

   _____

   (5.NBT.A.2)

NUMBER & OPERATIONS IN BASE TEN

6. A field is 10,000 feet long and 1,000 feet wide.

If there are fence posts every 20 feet along the edge of the field, all the way around the field, how many fence posts are there?

_____

(5.NBT.A.2)

7. In a long jump, Ryan jumped 17.26 feet. Tim jumped 17.262 feet. Alex jumped seventeen and twenty-five hundredths feet. Frank jumped seventeen and twenty-seven hundredths feet. Who jumped the farthest?

A. Ryan   **B.** Tim   **C.** Alex   **D.** Frank

(5.NBT.A.3)

8. Sandy scored a 92.3% on her test. Jackie scored a 92.03% on her test. Ben scored a 92.33% on his test. Carson scored a 93.31% on his test. Who had the lowest test score?

A. Sandy   **B.** Jackie   **C.** Ben   **D.** Carson

(5.NBT.A.3)

9. Michael is playing the NBA Live video game. He wants to select the player with the best free throw percentage.

  □ Marco Belinelli – Atlanta Hawks – 94.2%
  □ Stephen Curry – Golden State Warriors – 93.3%
  □ Jamal Crawford – Minnesota Timberwolves – 93.2%
  □ Damian Lillard – Portland Trail Blazers – 92.6%

Which of the following comparison statements is true?

A. Belinelli's percentage < Curry's percentage
B. Lillard's percentage > Crawford's percentage
C. Crawford's percentage > Curry's percentage
D. Curry's percentage > Lillard's percentage

(5.NBT.A.3)

NUMBER & OPERATIONS IN BASE TEN

10. There are 186 children coming to camp this summer. If one counselor is required for each 8 campers, how many counselors should be hired?

A. 24 **B.** 23 **C.** 25 **D.** 22

5.NBT.A.4

11. Which number has an odd hundredths digit but, when rounded to the nearest tenth, the tenths digit is even?

A. 2.12 **B.** 5.37 **C.** 2.33 **D.** 8.49

5.NBT.A.4

12. John has 8 ten-dollar bills. He is buying 2 shirts that are $27 and $14. How many bills should he give the clerk?

A. 4 bills **B.** 5 bills **C.** 2 bills **D.** 3 bills

5.NBT.A.4

13. A Ferris Wheel completes a rotation in 67 seconds. How many seconds will it take to complete 15 rotations?

A. 1,005 seconds **B.** 670 seconds
C. 335 seconds **D.** 82 seconds

5.NBT.B.5

14. An orange juice machine makes 6 glasses of juice from one bag of oranges. How many glasses of juice does the machine make from 12 bags?

A. 72 glasses **B.** 18 glasses
C. 60 glasses **D.** 66 glasses

5.NBT.B.5

prepaze

NUMBER & OPERATIONS IN BASE TEN

CHAPTER REVIEW

15. A team of football players spends 22 minutes on weight training every week. If their season is 32 weeks, how many minutes do they spend in the weight room during the entire season?

A. 600 minutes   **B.** 660 minutes
C. 704 minutes   **D.** 764 minutes

5.NBT.B.5

16. Elizabeth wrote and published a book about her teacher. The book has 15 pages. There are a total of 45 pictures in the book. If each page has the same number of pictures, how many pictures did she put on each page?

A. 1   **B.** 2   **C.** 3   **D.** 4

5.NBT.B.6

17. Which expression is equivalent to $4500 \div 50$?

A. $4500 \div 5$ **B.** $450 \div 5$ **C.** $5000 \div 50$ **D.** $500 \div 5$

5.NBT.B.6

18. What is the remainder of 122 divided by 5?

A. 2   **B.** 4   **C.** 6   **D.** 8

5.NBT.B.6

19. A store sells soccer balls for $8.99. If they sell 4,211 soccer balls in a season, about how much money do they make from soccer ball sales? Round the answer to the nearest 100.

5.NBT.B.7

prepaze

NUMBER & OPERATIONS IN BASE TEN

20. What number multiplied by 6 results in a product of 45.9?

_____

5.NBT.B.7

CHAPTER REVIEW

EXTRA PRACTICE

prepaze

NUMBER & OPERATIONS IN BASE TEN

1. A city weatherman is calculating the total rainfall for the three summer months. In June, it rained 2.37 inches. In July, it rained 1.8 inches. In August, it rained 18.37 inches. What is the total rainfall, in inches?

_____

(5.NBT.B.7)

2. Mary bought 8.7 pounds of raspberries and blueberries at the store. If 6.54 pounds were raspberries, how many pounds were blueberries?

_____

(5.NBT.B.7)

3. James went on a road trip. On the first day, he drove 455 miles, on the second day he drove 365 miles, and on the third day he drove 189 miles.

True or false: On the first and second day combined, James drove 10 times the distance that he drove on the third day.

A. True   **B.** False

(5.NBT.A.1)

4. A new shipment of fabric arrived at the fabric store. The shipment contained 10 rolls of white cotton fabric and each roll held 72.3 yards of fabric. The shipment also included 4 rolls of black cotton fabric and each roll held 112.3 yards of fabric.

True or false: In all, there was 10 times as much white cotton fabric as there was black cotton fabric.

A. True   **B.** False

(5.NBT.A.1)

NUMBER & OPERATIONS IN BASE TEN

5. Using the digits in the 6.394, fill in the blanks below.

    A. ones digit: _____

    B. tenths digit: _____

    C. hundredths digit: _____

    D. thousandths digit: _____

(5.NBT.A.1)

6. A building had 100 windows. If it takes 4.32 minutes to wash each window, it will take _____ hours to wash all 100 windows.

(5.NBT.A.2)

7. A garbage Dump was 100 feet long, 40 feet wide, and 40 feet deep. The volume of the inside of the garbage dump is _____ cubic feet.

(5.NBT.A.2)

8. A group of 7 students has to complete a total of 1,000 hours of community service for a scholarship program. If each student completed 6 hours of community service each day, it would take at least _____ days for all 1,000 hours to be completed.

(5.NBT.A.2)

9. Brandy planted a rose garden. She measured how much the flowers grew each day. Below are her measurements in inches. Rewrite the decimals in order from least to greatest.

0.111	0.101	0.110	0.011	0.112

(5.NBT.A.3)

prepaze

NUMBER & OPERATIONS IN BASE TEN

10. Dr. Smith poured partial liters of water into five beakers. Below are the amounts of water he poured into each beaker. Rewrite the decimals in order from greatest to least.

0.909	0.919	0.091	0.099	0.991

5.NBT.A.3

11. Find the percentage of the shaded area for each shape below. Which shape has the highest percentage of shaded area?

  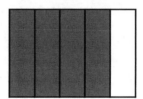 

A. Circle   **B.** Hexagon   **C.** Rectangle   **D.** Rhombus

5.NBT.A.3

12. There are 671 golf balls in a storage unit. You want to pack them in shipping boxes that hold 50 each. How many boxes do you need to pack all the golf balls.

5.NBT.A.4

NUMBER & OPERATIONS IN BASE TEN

13. Elise has five $20 bills. She buys 2 video games; one for $25.99 and one for $35.95. How many bills should she give the clerk?

_____

5.NBT.A.4

14. A question on Whitney's test requires her to round 3.23768 to the ten thousandth place. Her answer was 3.2378. She is incorrect. What should her answer have been?

_____

5.NBT.A.4

15. Two twins share a birthday party. Twenty-four of the guests at their party each bring 3 presents for each of them. How many presents are at the party?

_____

5.NBT.B.5

16. Mrs. Lawrence's class has 10 bags of candy. There are 20 pieces of candy in each bag. If there are 15 students in her class, does she have enough candy to give each child 15 pieces?

_____

5.NBT.B.5

17. If two factors are 72 and 5, what is the third factor of 11,520?

_____

5.NBT.B.5

prepaze

18. John bought 6 video games. Each game cost $35 on sale. If he gave the cashier $220, how much change will he get back?

_____

5.NBT.B.6

19. A farmer is packing apples into boxes. He puts 18 apples in each box. If he packs 12 boxes and has 9 extra apples remaining, how many apples did he start with?

_____

5.NBT.B.6

20. Ben divided 68 by 6. He said the quotient was 11 with a remainder of 6. Why was he incorrect?

_____

_____

_____

5.NBT.B.6

NUMBER & OPERATIONS FRACTIONS

prepaze

www.prepaze.com

NUMBER & OPERATIONS – FRACTIONS

1. What missing value makes these fractions equivalent? Solve for **x**.

$$\frac{3}{7} = \frac{x}{14}$$

A. 6 **B.** 7 **C.** 21 **D.** 42

5.NF.A.1

2. What missing value makes these fractions equivalent? Solve for **x**.

$$\frac{4}{9} = \frac{8}{x}$$

A. 4 **B.** 12 **C.** 18 **D.** 72

5.NF.A.1

3. Which response shows $4\frac{5}{6}$ as an improper fraction?

A. $\frac{9}{6}$ **B.** $\frac{20}{6}$ **C.** $\frac{24}{6}$ **D.** $\frac{29}{6}$

5.NF.A.1

4. Which response shows $\frac{17}{4}$ as a mixed number?

A. $4\frac{1}{4}$ **B.** $4\frac{3}{4}$ **C.** $17\frac{1}{4}$ **D.** $17\frac{3}{4}$

5.NF.A.1

5. Solve for **x**.

$$\frac{6}{11} + x = \frac{74}{55}$$

A. $\frac{2}{7}$ **B.** $\frac{4}{5}$ **C.** $\frac{3}{5}$ **D.** $\frac{5}{8}$

5.NF.A.1

prepaze

NUMBER & OPERATIONS – FRACTIONS

6. **True or False:**

$$\frac{5}{6} + \frac{3}{8} = \frac{67}{72}$$

    A. True   **B.** False

(5.NF.A.1)

7. **True or False:**

$$\frac{3}{5} - \frac{4}{9} = \frac{7}{45}$$

    A. True   **B.** False

(5.NF.A.1)

8. **True or False:**

$$6\frac{1}{2} = 1\frac{1}{2} + 5$$

    A. True   **B.** False

(5.NF.A.1)

9. **True or False:**

$$3\frac{1}{2} - 2\frac{1}{4} > 2\frac{1}{4}$$

    A. True   **B.** False

(5.NF.A.1)

10. Explain how $\frac{2}{3} + \frac{5}{4}$ is equivalent to $\frac{8}{12} + \frac{15}{12}$.

_____

_____

_____

(5.NF.A.1)

11. At a dinner party, a lasagna was equally shared among the dinner guests. If there were 14 people at the party, what fraction of the lasagna did each person get to eat?

    A. $\frac{1}{14}$ **B.** $\frac{2}{14}$ **C.** $\frac{3}{14}$ **D.** $\frac{4}{14}$

(5.NF.A.2)

12. Three friends ate an extra-large pizza. Ryan ate 4 slices, Cody ate 6, and Travis ate 3. If the pizza was equally cut into 16 slices, what fraction of the pizza was left over?

    A. $\frac{3}{16}$ **B.** $\frac{5}{16}$ **C.** $\frac{7}{16}$ **D.** $\frac{9}{16}$

(5.NF.A.2)

NUMBER & OPERATIONS – FRACTIONS

13. The cake recipe calls for $4\frac{1}{2}$ cups of flour. If the flour sack only has $2\frac{2}{3}$ cups of flour left in it, then what fraction of flour will still be needed?

A. $\frac{11}{6}$ cups   **B.** $\frac{13}{6}$ cups   **C.** $1\frac{5}{6}$ cups   **D.** A & C

5.NF.A.2

14. During the month of February, Matt grew $\frac{6}{7}$ of an inch while his brother Robert grew $\frac{3}{4}$ of an inch. How many inches did both brothers grow altogether during February?

A. $\frac{42}{28}$ inches   **B.** $\frac{43}{28}$ inches   **C.** $\frac{44}{28}$ inches   **D.** $\frac{45}{28}$ inches

5.NF.A.2

15. George drives 20 miles to work. Along the way, he drives $4\frac{1}{3}$ miles then stops at his favorite coffee shop. George drives another $8\frac{2}{7}$ miles then stops again at a gas station.

True or False: George still must drive $7\frac{8}{21}$ miles to get to work.

A. True   **B.** False

5.NF.A.2

16. Tiffany and Kelly share a chocolate bar. Tiffany eats $\frac{1}{6}$ of the chocolate bar. Kelly eats $\frac{2}{5}$ of the chocolate bar.

True or False: $\frac{13}{30}$ of the chocolate bar is left.

A. True   **B.** False

5.NF.A.2

prepaze

NUMBER & OPERATIONS – FRACTIONS

17. Carol makes a tray of brownies. Her mom eats $\frac{1}{12}$ of the tray. Her dad eats $\frac{1}{15}$ of the tray.

True or False: Together, her parents ate $\frac{2}{27}$ of the tray of brownies.

A. True   **B.** False

5.NF.A.2

18. Dustin went snowboarding. He went $\frac{1}{5}$ of the way down the hill. He stopped to catch his breath. Dustin then went another $\frac{3}{4}$ of the way down the hill.

True or False: Dustin snowboarded down $\frac{4}{9}$ of the hill.

A. True   **B.** False

5.NF.A.2

19. True and False: If Mr. Johnson had $\frac{1}{4}$ of the class work on math homework and $\frac{1}{3}$ of the class work on a reading assignment, then that means $\frac{1}{12}$ of the class worked on neither math nor reading.

A. True   **B.** False

5.NF.A.2

20. Amy jumped $7\frac{5}{6}$ feet in the long jump event. Andy jumped $9\frac{7}{8}$ feet in the same event. How many feet did both Amy and Andy jump together?

A. $\frac{850}{48}$ feet   **B.** $17\frac{17}{24}$ feet   **C.** $17\frac{32}{48}$ feet   **D.** A & B

5.NF.A.2

UNIT 2:   FRACTION MULTIPLICATION

NUMBER & OPERATIONS – FRACTIONS

1. Rewrite the fraction $\frac{5}{9}$ as a division problem.

A. $5 \div 9$ **B.** 9×5

C. 5×9 **D.** $9 \div 5$

5.NF.B.3

2. Rewrite the fraction $\frac{9}{4}$ as a division problem.

A. 9×4 **B.** $9 \div 4$

C. 4×9 **D.** $4 \div 9$

5.NF.B.3

3. Find the fraction of the shaded area in the shape below. Rewrite the fraction as a division problem.

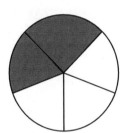

A. 5×2 **B.** $2 \div 5$

C. 2×5 **D.** $5 \div 2$

5.NF.B.3

4. Find the fraction of the shaded area in the shape below. Rewrite the fraction as a division problem.

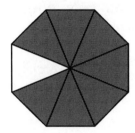

A. 1×8 **B.** $8 \div 1$

C. 7×8 **D.** $7 \div 8$

5.NF.B.3

5. Parker walked the dog $\frac{21}{13}$ miles. Rewrite the fraction as a division problem.

A. $13 \div 21$ **B.** $21 \div 13$ **C.** $8 \div 13$ **D.** $8 \div 21$

5.NF.B.3

FRACTION MULTIPLICATION

NUMBER & OPERATIONS – FRACTIONS

FRACTION MULTIPLICATION

6. Simplify: $8 \times \frac{1}{7}$

A. $\frac{9}{7}$ **B.** $\frac{8}{7}$

C. $1\frac{1}{7}$ **D.** B & C

5.NF.B.4

7. Simplify: $\frac{4}{6} \times \frac{1}{5}$

A. $\frac{2}{15}$ **B.** $\frac{20}{6}$

C. $\frac{5}{11}$ **D.** $\frac{5}{30}$

5.NF.B.4

8. Simplify: $\frac{6}{7} \times \frac{2}{9}$

A. $\frac{8}{16}$ **B.** $\frac{14}{54}$ **C.** $\frac{4}{21}$ **D.** $\frac{8}{63}$

5.NF.B.4

9. The bakery needed to bake 9 cakes for a holiday event. If each cake would be decorated with $\frac{7}{8}$ of a can of frosting, at least how many cans of frosting would the bakery need?

A. 7 cans   **B.** 8 cans   **C.** 9 cans   **D.** 10 cans

5.NF.B.4

10. There are 6 boys at the movie theater. If each boy eats $\frac{4}{9}$ of a bucket of popcorn, at least how many buckets of popcorn should be ordered?

A. 1 bucket   **B.** 2 buckets   **C.** 3 buckets   **D.** 4 buckets

5.NF.B.4

11. True or False: $9\frac{1}{4} \times \frac{1}{4} > 9\frac{1}{4}$

A. True   **B.** False

5.NF.B.5

12. True or False: $1\frac{2}{3} = 1\frac{3}{10}$

A. True   **B.** False

5.NF.B.5

NUMBER & OPERATIONS – FRACTIONS

13. True or False: This model can be used to prove $\frac{3}{4} > \frac{2}{4}$.

A. True   **B.** False

5.NF.B.5

14. Is $5 \times \frac{2}{7}$ greater or less than 5? Explain your answer below.

_____

_____

_____

5.NF.B.5

15. Is $8 \times \frac{6}{5}$ greater or less than 8? Explain your answer below.

_____

_____

_____

5.NF.B.5

16. Drew collected 28 shells on the beach. If $\frac{1}{4}$ of the shells were white, how many of the shells were white?

A. 5 shells   **B.** 6 shells   **C.** 7 shells   **D.** 8 shells

5.NF.B.6

FRACTION MULTIPLICATION

NUMBER & OPERATIONS – FRACTIONS

17. The jar of cookies was $\frac{2}{3}$ full. If Isabella and her friends ate $\frac{1}{6}$ of the remaining cookies, what fraction of the entire jar of cookies did Isabella and her friends eat?

   A. $\frac{1}{9}$ of the jar of cookies   **B.** $\frac{2}{9}$ of the jar of cookies

   C. $\frac{1}{18}$ of the jar of cookies   **D.** $\frac{3}{18}$ of the jar of cookies

5.NF.B.6

18. Marci mixed $2\frac{4}{5}$ teaspoons of spices into a batch of cookies. If she made 45 batches, how many teaspoons of spices did Marci use in all?

   A. 120 teaspoons   **B.** 126 teaspoons
   C. 130 teaspoons   **D.** 136 teaspoons

5.NF.B.6

19. Mr. Davidson ordered $4\frac{2}{7}$ pounds of fish to make dinner. If he only needed $\frac{4}{9}$ of what he originally ordered, how many pounds of fish would be used?

   A. $1\frac{1}{9}$ pounds 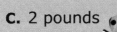   **B.** $1\frac{19}{21}$ pounds

   C. 2 pounds   **D.** 3 pounds

5.NF.B.6

20. The dentist used $3\frac{1}{3}$ tubes of toothpaste a day. How many total tubes of toothpaste did the dentist use in a period of 12 days?

   A. 36 tubes of toothpaste   **B.** 38 tubes of toothpaste
   C. 40 tubes of toothpaste   **D.** 42 tubes of toothpaste

5.NF.B.6

UNIT 3: FRACTION DIVISION

NUMBER & OPERATIONS – FRACTIONS

1. Simplify: $\frac{3}{4} \div 6 =$ _____

   5.NBT.B.7

2. Simplify: $\frac{6}{7} \div 5 =$ _____

   5.NBT.B.7

3. Simplify: $\frac{5}{6} \div 3 =$ _____

   5.NBT.B.7

4. Simplify: $\frac{4}{9} \div 8 =$ _____

   5.NBT.B.7

5. Simplify: $\frac{3}{8} \div 2 =$ _____

   5.NBT.B.7

6. Simplify: $\frac{2}{7} \div 9 =$ _____

   5.NBT.B.7

7. Simplify: $2 \div \frac{3}{5} =$ _____

   5.NBT.B.7

8. Simplify: $8 \div \frac{3}{5} =$ _____

   5.NBT.B.7

9. A group of 3 friends went to the candy store to buy some chocolate treats. How much chocolate will each friend get if all 3 share $\frac{1}{2}$ pound of chocolate equally?

   A. $\frac{2}{6}$ pound of chocolate   **B.** $\frac{1}{6}$ pound of chocolate

   C. $\frac{1}{18}$ pound of chocolate   **D.** $\frac{3}{12}$ pound of chocolate

   5.NBT.B.7

prepaze

NUMBER & OPERATIONS – FRACTIONS

FRACTION DIVISION

10. There was $\frac{1}{5}$ of an apple pie leftover from the dinner party. If the pie was divided equally among 6 people, what fraction of the pie will each person get to eat?

A. $\frac{1}{11}$ of the apple pie   **B.** $\frac{1}{20}$ of the apple pie

C. $\frac{1}{30}$ of the apple pie   **D.** $\frac{1}{2}$ of the apple pie

(5.NBT.B.7)

11. There was $\frac{2}{3}$ of a pitcher of lemonade in the refrigerator. If the lemonade is shared equally among 5 friends, what fraction of the pitcher would each friend have to drink?

A. $\frac{1}{15}$ of the pitcher   **B.** $\frac{2}{15}$ of the pitcher

C. $\frac{3}{15}$ of the pitcher   **D.** $\frac{4}{15}$ of the pitcher

(5.NBT.B.7)

12. Ms. Johnson wanted $\frac{3}{4}$ of her patio deck painted. If she hired 4 painters to do the job, what fraction of the patio deck would each painter paint?

A. $\frac{1}{16}$ of the patio deck   **B.** $\frac{3}{16}$ of the patio deck

C. $\frac{3}{8}$ of the patio deck   **D.** $\frac{1}{8}$ of the patio deck

(5.NBT.B.7)

13. Isabella purchased a bag of raisins to pack into her boxed lunches. If she was to divide the raisins into smaller-sized bags, how many $\frac{1}{3}$ cup servings could she get out of 2 cups of raisins?

A. $\frac{1}{6}$ servings   **B.** 4 servings

C. 5 servings   **D.** 6 servings

(5.NBT.B.7)

NUMBER & OPERATIONS – FRACTIONS

14. Oliver went on an 8-mile hike. If Oliver stopped to take a picture at every $\frac{1}{6}$ mile, how many pictures did Oliver take?

    A. 45 pictures   **B.** 46 pictures   **C.** 47 pictures   **D.** 48 pictures

5.NBT.B.7

15. Megan reads the same amount each night for 6 nights in a row. After 6 nights, she had read $\frac{1}{2}$ of a book.

True or False: This means that Megan read $\frac{1}{12}$ of the book each night.

    A. True   **B.** False

5.NBT.B.7

16. Jeff has a bag of rice. He scoops out 6 cups of rice to make a pot of fried rice.

True or False: There are 12 servings total if each serving is $\frac{1}{2}$ cup.

    A. True   **B.** False

5.NBT.B.7

17. Four friends go to the movies. They share $\frac{1}{2}$ lb. of popcorn equally.

True or False: Each person gets $\frac{1}{6}$ of the bag of popcorn.

    A. True   **B.** False

5.NBT.B.7

18. Julie wants to make 2 Halloween costumes from a piece of fabric that is $\frac{1}{4}$ yard long.

True or False: She will have to use $\frac{1}{8}$ yard of fabric for each costume.

    A. True   **B.** False

5.NBT.B.7

prepaze

NUMBER & OPERATIONS – FRACTIONS

19. Ms. Taylor is making two cakes. She uses $\frac{1}{3}$ cup of sugar in all.

True or False: That means Ms. Taylor used $\frac{1}{8}$ cup of sugar in each cake.

A. True   **B.** False

5.NBT.B.7

20. A group of fifth grade students ran a 3-mile relay race. Each student ran $\frac{1}{4}$ of a mile.

True or False: 12 students participated in the race. Use the visual fraction model below to help you.

3 miles											
1/4	1/4	1/4	1/4	1/4	1/4	1/4	1/4	1/4	1/4	1/4	1/4

A. True   **B.** False

5.NBT.B.7

CHAPTER REVIEW

NUMBER & OPERATIONS – FRACTIONS

1. Solve for x

$$\frac{2}{9} - x = \frac{1}{18}$$

A. $\frac{2}{13}$ **B.** $\frac{1}{5}$ **C.** $\frac{1}{4}$ **D.** $\frac{1}{6}$

5.NF.A.1

2. Solve for x.

$$x - 2\frac{4}{9} = 4\frac{12}{135}$$

A. $3\frac{4}{15}$ **B.** $4\frac{5}{15}$

C. $5\frac{4}{15}$ **D.** $6\frac{8}{15}$

5.NF.A.1

3. Solve for x.

$$3\frac{1}{5} + x = 3\frac{4}{5}$$

A. $\frac{1}{5}$ **B.** $\frac{2}{5}$

C. $\frac{3}{5}$ **D.** $\frac{4}{5}$

5.NF.A.1

4. There is 8 feet of wrapping paper on the roll. Jennifer needs $3\frac{1}{6}$ feet of wrapping paper. What fraction of the wrapping paper would be left over?

A. $4\frac{5}{6}$ feet **B.** $4\frac{4}{6}$ feet

C. $4\frac{3}{6}$ feet **D.** $4\frac{2}{6}$ feet

5.NF.A.2

5. Katie and Ben walked $\frac{7}{9}$ of a mile to the grocery store. They then walked another $\frac{4}{7}$ of a mile to the movie theater. How many miles did both Katie and Ben walk in total?

A. $1\frac{20}{63}$ miles **B.** $1\frac{21}{63}$ miles

C. $1\frac{22}{63}$ miles **D.** $1\frac{23}{63}$ miles

5.NF.A.2

prepaze

NUMBER & OPERATIONS – FRACTIONS

6. The dog drank $7\frac{1}{8}$ cups of water in the morning and $5\frac{1}{4}$ cups of water in the evening. How many cups of water did the dog drink in all that day?

   A. $12\frac{12}{32}$ cups   **B.** $12\frac{3}{8}$ cups   **C.** $\frac{396}{32}$ cups   **D.** All of the above

   5.NF.A.2

7. Twenty-four brownies were equally shared among 6 friends. How many brownies did each friend get?

   Write the division problem: _____.

   Now write the division problem in the form of a fraction: _____.

   5.NF.B.3

8. There were 18 cups of sugar split equally into 10 pies. How many cups of sugar did each pie get?

   Write the division problem: _____.

   Now write the division problem in the form of a fraction: _____.

   5.NF.B.3

9. After a busy day at the ice cream shop, there were only 8 scoops of ice cream left. If the scoops were split equally among the last 5 customers, each customer got _____ scoops of ice cream.

   5.NF.B.3

10. Mr. Harry wants to put down a piece of material to protect the bottom of his tool box. If the bottom of the box was $\frac{1}{3}$ feet long and $\frac{5}{6}$ feet wide, what is the area that needs to be covered?

   A. $\frac{6}{9}$ **B.** $\frac{5}{18}$ **C.** $\frac{6}{18}$ **D.** $\frac{5}{9}$

   5.NF.B.4

NUMBER & OPERATIONS – FRACTIONS

11. The garden is 12 yards long and $10\frac{1}{2}$ yards wide. How many yards of soil will be needed to cover the area of the garden?

A. 126 square yards of soil. **B.** 60 square yards of soil.
C. 120 square yards of soil. **D.** 11 square yards of soil.

(5.NF.B.4)

12. True or False: $5 \times \frac{6}{7} = \frac{30}{7}$

A. True **B.** False

(5.NF.B.4)

13. Bethenny washed $\frac{2}{5}$ of the dirty clothes on the top $\frac{1}{2}$ of the laundry basket. Decide whether Bethenny did more or less than $\frac{2}{5}$ of the full load of laundry.

_____

_____

_____

(5.NF.B.5)

14. Mrs. Brown has a driveway that is $13\frac{1}{3}$ feet long and $6\frac{1}{3}$ feet wide. Mr. Green has a driveway that is $7\frac{1}{3}$ feet long and $12\frac{1}{3}$ feet wide. Compare the areas of the two driveways. Which neighbor has the larger driveway? Explain your answer below.

_____

_____

_____

(5.NF.B.5)

prepaze

NUMBER & OPERATIONS – FRACTIONS

15. Max bought 14 roses for his girlfriend on Valentine's Day. If $\frac{1}{7}$ of the boutique was made up of purple roses, how many of the roses were purple?

A. 1 **B.** 2 **C.** 3 **D.** 4

5.NF.B.5

16. Ms. Smith has a backyard garden. She divided the garden in half. One half of the garden is planted with berries. She planted $\frac{1}{6}$ of this half with blueberries. Look at the diagram below. How much of the garden is planted with blueberries?

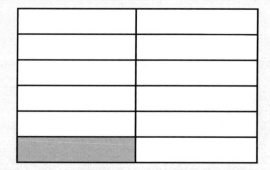

A. $\frac{1}{2}$ of the garden is planted with blueberries.

B. $\frac{1}{4}$ of the garden is planted with blueberries.

C. $\frac{1}{6}$ of the garden is planted with blueberries.

D. $\frac{1}{12}$ of the garden is planted with blueberries.

5.NF.B.6

17. Samantha is making a dozen cupcakes. The recipe she is using makes 24 cupcakes. It calls for $\frac{1}{2}$ teaspoon of vanilla.

True or False: If she splits the recipe in half, she would need $\frac{1}{4}$ teaspoon of vanilla.

A. True **B.** False

5.NF.B.6

NUMBER & OPERATIONS – FRACTIONS

18. Julia is making a quilt. Each quilt square is $4\frac{1}{2}$ inches wide and $3\frac{1}{4}$ inches long.

True or False: The area each quilt square will cover is 15 square inches.

A. True   **B.** False

5.NF.B.6

19. Simplify: $5 \div \frac{4}{9} =$ _____

5.NF.B.7

20. Simplify: $7 \div \frac{8}{9} =$ _____

5.NF.B.7

EXTRA PRACTICE

prepaze

NUMBER & OPERATIONS – FRACTIONS

1. Holly wanted to paint her house. She had $9\frac{5}{6}$ gallons of paint left. Holly accidently knocked over a can of paint. She had spilled $2\frac{1}{2}$ gallons onto the garage floor.

True or False: Holly now has $7\frac{6}{12}$ gallons of paint left.

A. True   **B.** False

(5.NF.A.1)

2. Three people competed in a pie eating contest. When time was called, each competitor had eaten three-fourths of the pie in front of them. Name three fractions that are equivalent to $\frac{3}{4}$.

_____

(5.NF.A.1)

3. Three students were taking a test. After the teacher had graded each student's test, all three students had correctly answered fourth-fifths of the questions. Name three fractions that are equivalent to $\frac{4}{5}$.

_____

(5.NF.A.1)

4. The difference between **x** and **y** is: _____.

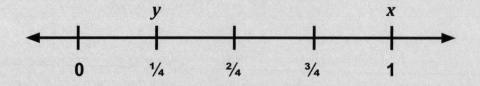

(5.NF.A.2)

NUMBER & OPERATIONS – FRACTIONS

5. The difference between *x* and *y* is: _____.

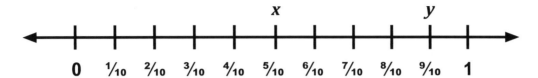

5.NF.A.2

6. Mr. Johnson had $\frac{4}{9}$ of the class work on math homework and $\frac{3}{8}$ of the class work on a reading assignment

True or False: $\frac{13}{72}$ of the class worked on neither math nor reading.

A. True   **B.** False

5.NF.A.2

7. Mrs. Smith made 14 quarts of punch. If she wanted to pour the punch equally into 3 punch bowls, each bowl would get _____ quarts of punch.

5.NF.B.3

8. Mark had 125 tennis balls. If he wanted to split them equally into 5 buckets, each bucket would have _____ tennis balls.

5.NF.B.3

9. Lucas worked at a movie theater. If he had 6 pounds of candy that he wanted to equally put into 22 bags, each bag would have _____ pounds of candy.

5.NF.B.3

prepaze

NUMBER & OPERATIONS – FRACTIONS

10. At the party, $\frac{4}{5}$ of the people there were children. Of the children, $\frac{3}{4}$ were under the age of 5 years old.

True or False: This means that $\frac{3}{5}$ of the people at the party were children under the age of 5.

A. True **B.** False

(5.NF.B.4)

11. A patio table has a length of $3\frac{1}{4}$ meters and a width of $2\frac{3}{5}$ meters.

True or False: This means that $8\frac{6}{20}$ square meters is the area that will need to be covered by a tablecloth.

A. True **B.** False

(5.NF.B.4)

12. Samuel wanted to paint a piece of canvas navy blue. The piece of canvas was $9\frac{1}{8}$ inches tall and $6\frac{2}{3}$ inches wide.

True or False: This means that more than 60 square inches is the area that he will need to cover in paint.

A. True **B.** False

(5.NF.B.4)

13. Teresa needed to buy $4\frac{3}{7}$ yards of ribbon. Which of the lengths below is less than the amount of ribbon Teresa needs to buy?

A. $4\frac{4}{7}$ yards of ribbon **B.** $4\frac{5}{7}$ yards of ribbon

C. $4\frac{2}{7}$ yards of ribbon **D.** $4\frac{6}{7}$ yards of ribbon

(5.NF.B.5)

NUMBER & OPERATIONS – FRACTIONS

EXTRA PRACTICE

14. Using the number line below, what is the value of *x*?

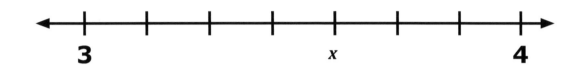

A. 3   **B.** $3\frac{3}{7}$ **C.** $3\frac{4}{7}$ **D.** $3\frac{5}{7}$

5.NF.B.5

15. Tony studied for his final exams for $4\frac{2}{5}$ hours every afternoon. After $10\frac{7}{8}$ days, how many total hours has Tony studied for his exams?

A. Between 44 and 45 hours

B. Between 45 and 46 hours

C. Between 46 and 47 hours

D. Between 47 and 48 hours

5.NF.B.5

16. The tablecloth is $6\frac{1}{4}$ feet long on all four sides.

True or False: The area the tablecloth covers is 25 feet square.

A. True   **B.** False

5.NF.B.6

17. The plant grew $\frac{1}{12}$ inches every day.

True or False: After 20 days, the plant grew over 2 inches.

A. True   **B.** False

5.NF.B.6

prepaze

NUMBER & OPERATIONS – FRACTIONS

18. Joey grew $3\frac{1}{6}$ inches every year for 4 years straight.

True or False: Joey grew a total of 13 inches after a period of 4 years.

A. True   **B.** False

5.NF.B.6

19. Henry has 12 feet of fence. He wants to install a post every $\frac{1}{3}$ feet.

True or False: Henry will need to put up 36 posts.

A. True   **B.** False

5.NF.B.7

20. Jill had 10 yards of fabric that she used to make scarves for her friends. If each scarf she made was $\frac{5}{7}$ of a yard long, how many friends would be able to get a scarf?

A. 10 friends   **B.** 13 friends
C. 14 friends   **D.** 15 friends

5.NF.B.7

MEASUREMENT & DATA

prepaze

www.prepaze.com

MEASUREMENT & DATA

1. Ivan measures 5 different insects he found in a park. This table shows the length of each insect.

Insect	Length (centimeters)
Grasshopper	9.05
Ant	0.67
Ladybug	1.48
Beetle	2.48
Pill bug	0.25

What is the combined length of these insects in meters?

A. 1.393 meters

B. 13.93 meters

C. 0.1393 meters

D. 1,393 meters

5.MD.A.1

2. Jerrod is 5 feet 5 inches tall. His brother is 8 inches taller. What is the height of Jerrod's brother?

A. 6 feet 13 inches

B. 6 feet 1 inch

C. 4 feet 9 inches

D. 5 feet 1 inch

5.MD.A.1

3. Li compares the lengths of 5 different pencils. Each pencil has an eraser which is 0.65 centimeters long. This table shows the length of each pencil, including the eraser.

Pencil	Length (centimeters)
A	11.1
B	14.6
C	12.1
D	15.9
E	15

Which pencils are between 110 and 145 millimeters long without the eraser?

A. Pencils B, C, E

B. Pencils B and C

C. Pencils A, B, and C

D. Pencils A and C

5.MD.A.1

prepaze

MEASUREMENT & DATA

CONVERSION OF MEASUREMENTS

4. Ava measures 4 different insects she found in a park. This table shows the length of each insect.

Insect	Length (centimeters)
Ant	11.1
Cricket	14.6
Grasshopper	12.1
Fly	15.9

What is the combined length of these insects in meters?

A. 5.37 meters

B. 53.7 meters

C. 537 meters

D. 0.537 meters

5.MD.A.1

5. Maha is 4 feet 9 inches tall. Her sister is 10 inches shorter. What is the height of Maha's sister?

    A. 4 feet 1 inch   **B.** 3 feet 11 inches

    C. 5 feet 7 inches   **D.** 3 feet 7 inches

5.MD.A.1

6. Mario and Lulu are on the same baseball team. Mario's bat is 31 inches, and Lulu's bat is 29 inches. How much shorter is Lulu's bat than Mario's bat.

    A. 2 feet   **B.** $\frac{2}{3}$ foot   **C.** $\frac{1}{6}$ foot   **D.** 0.2 foot

5.MD.A.1

7. Micah and Oscar measure their height in inches. Oscar is $\frac{3}{4}$ foot taller than Micah. Which choice could be their heights?

    A. Micah: 4 feet 6 inches   Oscar: 5 feet 3 inches

    B. Micah: 5 feet 1-inch   Oscar: 5 feet 4 inches

    C. Micah: 5 feet   Oscar: 4 feet 3 inches

    D. Micah: 4 feet 9 inches   Oscar: 5 feet 3 inches

5.MD.A.1

MEASUREMENT & DATA

8. Jesse has 4 books which have a combined mass of 6.78 kilograms. Two of the books have a mass of 594 grams. What is the mass of the remaining two books, in grams?

A. 84 grams   **B.** 6,186 grams   **C.** 6.78 grams   **D.** 7,374 grams

5.MD.A.1

9. Oliver has 3 books which have a combined mass of 4.35 kilograms. Each book is the same mass. What is the mass of one book in grams?

A. 1.45 grams   **B.** 13.05 grams   **C.** 1,450 grams   **D.** 13,050 grams

5.MD.A.1

10. One sheet of paper is $8\frac{1}{2}$ inches wide and 11 inches long. How many pieces of paper are needed to cover a floor which is $14\frac{1}{6}$ feet wide and $18\frac{1}{3}$ feet long?

A. 20   **B.** 400   **C.** 40   **D.** 250

5.MD.A.1

11. One tile is 4 inches wide and 6 inches long. How many tiles are needed to cover a floor which is $8\frac{1}{3}$ feet wide and $12\frac{1}{2}$ feet long?

A. 25   **B.** 50   **C.** 250   **D.** 625

5.MD.A.1

12. Emile fills a fish tank with a capacity of 36 liters $\frac{3}{4}$ full. How many milliliters of empty space remains in the fish tank?

A. 900   **B.** 9,000   **C.** 2,700   **D.** 27,000

5.MD.A.1

prepaze

MEASUREMENT & DATA

13. A large tub holds 30 gallons of water. When the tub is full, it drains at a speed of 40 quarts per minute. How many minutes does it take to drain a full tub?

_____

(5.MD.A.1)

14. A water jug contains 30 pints of water. How many cups of water are in this jug?

_____

(5.MD.A.1)

15. Alicia has a gallon of milk, and she pours 8 ounces of milk into each glass. How many glasses does Alicia use?

_____

(5.MD.A.1)

16. A shoe company produces 375 feet of shoelaces every hour. Each shoelace is 30 inches long. How many shoelaces are produced in 3 hours?

_____

(5.MD.A.1)

17. Dara is wrapping 12 gifts. Each gift requires 24 inches of ribbon. She has 7.5 feet of ribbon. How many more inches of ribbon does Dara need to finish wrapping the gifts?

(5.MD.A.1)

MEASUREMENT & DATA

18. John, Riley, Peter, and Theo are competing in a 3200-meter race. Each person runs the same distance. How many kilometers does each person run?

_____

5.MD.A.1

19. This table shows the weight of 4 containers of berries.

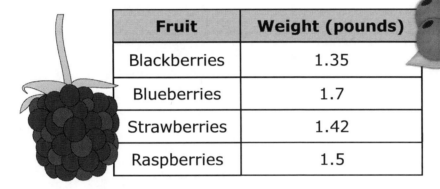

Fruit	Weight (pounds)
Blackberries	1.35
Blueberries	1.7
Strawberries	1.42
Raspberries	1.5

What is the total number of ounces in all 4 containers of berries? Do not round. Explain your reasoning.

_____

_____

_____

_____

_____

_____

5.MD.A.1

CONVERSION OF MEASUREMENTS

prepaze

MEASUREMENT & DATA

20. This table shows the weight of 4 containers of berries.

Fruit	Weight (pounds)
Strawberries	1.55
Blackberries	1.38
Raspberries	1.2
Blueberries	1.39

Edward estimates the 4 containers weigh a total of 64 ounces. Do you agree with Edward? Explain your reasoning.

_____

_____

_____

_____

_____

_____

5.MD.A.1

MEASUREMENT & DATA

1. Tia measures the lengths of some insects. The table shows her data.

$\frac{1}{2}$ inch, $\frac{1}{8}$ inch, $\frac{1}{4}$ inch, $\frac{1}{4}$ inch, $\frac{1}{2}$ inch

$\frac{1}{8}$ inch, $\frac{1}{4}$ inch, $\frac{1}{2}$ inch, $\frac{1}{8}$ inch, $\frac{1}{2}$ inch

$\frac{1}{4}$ inch, $\frac{1}{2}$ inch, $\frac{1}{8}$ inch, $\frac{1}{4}$ inch, $\frac{1}{4}$ inch

Tia is making a line plot for the data. How many data points will represent the insects that are $\frac{1}{2}$ inch long?

A. 4   **B.** 5   **C.** 15   **D.** 1

5.MD.B.2

2. Katy measures the lengths of some insects. The table shows her data.

$\frac{1}{4}$ inch, $\frac{1}{2}$ inch, $\frac{1}{4}$ inch, $\frac{1}{4}$ inch, $\frac{1}{8}$ inch

$\frac{1}{2}$ inch, $\frac{1}{4}$ inch, $\frac{1}{2}$ inch, $\frac{1}{4}$ inch, $\frac{1}{8}$ inch

$\frac{1}{2}$ inch, $\frac{1}{8}$ inch, $\frac{1}{8}$ inch, $\frac{1}{2}$ inch, $\frac{1}{4}$ inch

Katy is making a line plot for the data. How many data points will represent the insects that are $\frac{1}{4}$ inch long?

A. 15   **B.** 4   **C.** 6   **D.** 1

5.MD.B.2

prepaze

MEASUREMENT & DATA

3. This line plot displays the data collected on some insects.

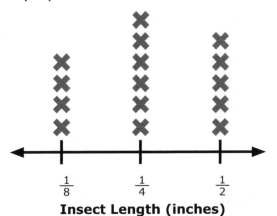

Insect Length (inches)

What is the combined length of the insects that are $\frac{1}{4}$ inch long?

A. $1\frac{1}{2}$ inches   **B.** 6 inches   **C.** $\frac{4}{6}$ inches   **D.** $\frac{6}{24}$ inches

(5.MD.B.2)

4. This line plot displays the data collected on some insects.

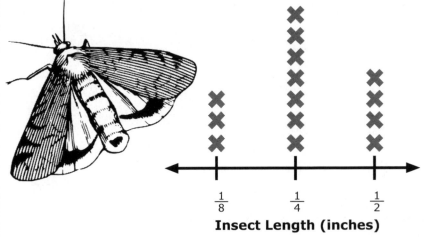

Insect Length (inches)

What is the combined length of the insects that are $\frac{1}{2}$ inch long?

A. $\frac{2}{4}$ inch   **B.** $\frac{1}{8}$ inch   **C.** 4 inches   **D.** 2 inches

(5.MD.B.2)

MEASUREMENT & DATA

5. This line plot displays the data collected on some dogs.

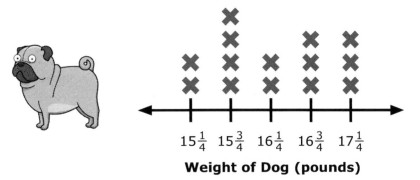

Weight of Dog (pounds)

What is the difference between the weight of the heaviest dogs and the lightest dogs?

A. $2\frac{1}{4}$ pounds   **B.** $\frac{2}{4}$ pounds   **C.** 2 pounds   **D.** 1 pound

5.MD.B.2

6. This line plot displays the data collected on some dogs.

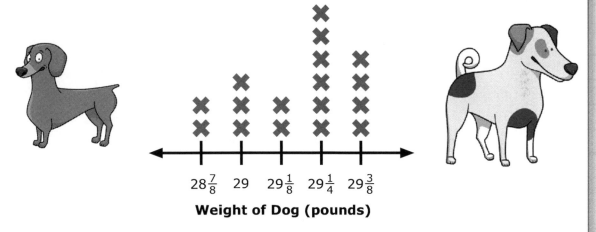

Weight of Dog (pounds)

What is the difference between the weight of the heaviest dogs and the lightest dogs?

A. $\frac{1}{2}$ pound   **B.** 1 pound   **C.** $\frac{3}{8}$ pound   **D.** 2 pounds

5.MD.B.2

prepaze

MEASUREMENT & DATA

7. Which line plot best represents the ages of the students in a fifth-grade class?

A.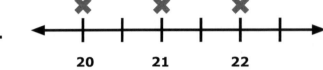

20   21   22

Students

B.

9   10   11

Students' Age

C.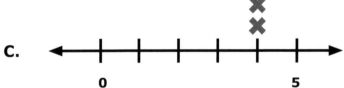

0   5

Grade Level

D.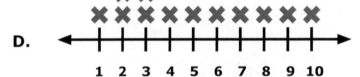

1   2   3   4   5   6   7   8   9   10

Students' Age

5.MD.B.2

MEASUREMENT & DATA

8. This line plot shows the age range of the students in Mrs. Green's class.

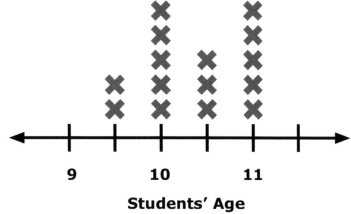

Students' Age

How many students are $10\frac{1}{2}$ years old?

A. 4   **B.** 5   **C.** 3   **D.** 1

5.MD.B.2

9. This line plot shows the age range of the students in Mr. Brown's class.

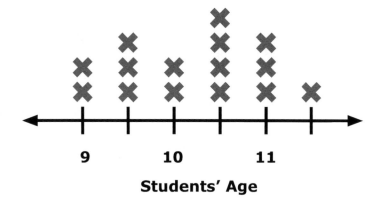

Students' Age

How many students are between $9\frac{1}{2}$ and 11 years old?

A. 12   **B.** 2   **C.** 4   **D.** 6

5.MD.B.2

prepaze

MEASUREMENT & DATA

GRAPHS AND DATA INTERPRETATION

10. This list shows the number of miles a deer travels each day.

$$10\tfrac{1}{2}, \ 12\tfrac{1}{4}, \ 20\tfrac{1}{8}, \ 12\tfrac{1}{4}, \ 11\tfrac{3}{8}, \ 13\tfrac{1}{2},$$

$$10\tfrac{1}{2}, \ 11\tfrac{5}{8}, \ 14\tfrac{1}{4}$$

Grady is making a line plot of this data. How many data points will be on the line plot?

A. 9   **B.** 7   **C.** 10   **D.** 2

(5.MD.B.2)

11. This list shows the number of miles Owen runs each day during part of January.

$$2\tfrac{1}{8}, \ 2\tfrac{7}{8}, \ 2\tfrac{1}{8}, \ 3\tfrac{1}{4}, \ 1\tfrac{5}{8}, \ 2\tfrac{7}{8}, \ 2\tfrac{7}{8}, \ 3\tfrac{3}{4}, \ 1\tfrac{5}{8}$$

$$2\tfrac{7}{8}, \ 3\tfrac{3}{4}, \ 2, \ 1\tfrac{5}{8}$$

Owen is making a line plot of this data. How many data points will be on the line plot?

A. 6   **B.** 7   **C.** 13   **D.** 4

(5.MD.B.2)

12. Dr. Adalumo uses this line plot to display the amount of growth his patients have had in one year.

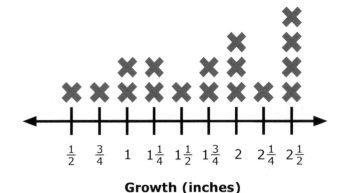

Growth (inches)

How many of Dr. Adalumo's patients grew more than 1 inch?

A. 13   **B.** 15

C. 17   **D.** 6

(5.MD.B.2)

MEASUREMENT & DATA

13. This list contains data collected on the distances walked by 15 people.

$$\frac{3}{2} \text{ miles}, \ \frac{3}{8} \text{ mile}, \ \frac{5}{4} \text{ miles}, \ \frac{7}{4} \text{ miles}, \ \frac{1}{2} \text{ mile}$$

$$\frac{6}{8} \text{ mile}, \ \frac{3}{4} \text{ mile}, \ \frac{3}{2} \text{ miles}, \ \frac{5}{8} \text{ mile}, \ \frac{1}{2} \text{ mile}$$

$$\frac{5}{4} \text{ miles}, \ \frac{7}{2} \text{ miles}, \ \frac{1}{8} \text{ mile}, \ \frac{7}{4} \text{ miles}, \ \frac{5}{4} \text{ miles}$$

Which distance will have the greatest number of data points on a line plot?

_____

5.MD.B.2

14. This list contains data collected about the weights of 10 cats.

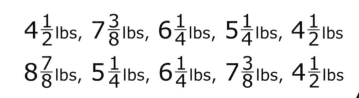

$$4\frac{1}{2}\text{lbs}, \ 7\frac{3}{8}\text{lbs}, \ 6\frac{1}{4}\text{lbs}, \ 5\frac{1}{4}\text{lbs}, \ 4\frac{1}{2}\text{lbs}$$

$$8\frac{7}{8}\text{lbs}, \ 5\frac{1}{4}\text{lbs}, \ 6\frac{1}{4}\text{lbs}, \ 7\frac{3}{8}\text{lbs}, \ 4\frac{1}{2}\text{lbs}$$

Which weight will have the fewest number of data points on a line plot?

_____

5.MD.B.2

prepaze

MEASUREMENT & DATA

GRAPHS AND DATA
INTERPRETATION

15. This line plot displays data collected on the length of 12 leaves.

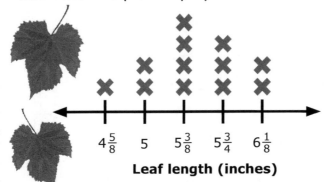

Leaf length (inches)

What is the combined length of the leaves that are $5\frac{3}{8}$ inches long?

_____

5.MD.B.2

16. This line plot displays data collected on the length of 12 leaves.

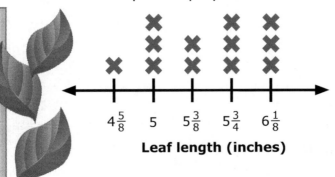

Leaf length (inches)

What is the difference between the length of the longest leaf and the shortest leaf?

_____

5.MD.B.2

17. This line plot shows the temperature recorded in Florida over 11 days.

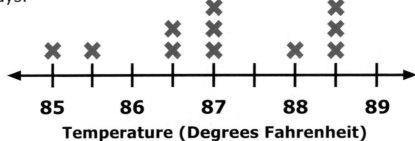

85   86   87   88   89
Temperature (Degrees Fahrenheit)

What is the difference between the highest and the lowest temperatures?

_____

5.MD.B.2

MEASUREMENT & DATA

18. This list includes data collected about the length of some insects.

$\frac{3}{4}$ inch, $\frac{5}{4}$ inch, $\frac{6}{4}$ inch, $\frac{7}{4}$ inch, $\frac{2}{4}$ inch

$\frac{3}{4}$ inch, $\frac{3}{4}$ inch, $\frac{6}{4}$ inch, $\frac{4}{4}$ inch, $\frac{5}{4}$ inch

$\frac{5}{4}$ inch, $\frac{7}{4}$ inch, $\frac{8}{4}$ inch, $\frac{6}{4}$ inch, $\frac{5}{4}$ inch

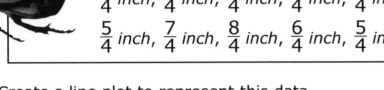

Create a line plot to represent this data.

(5.MD.B.2)

19. This list shows the number of miles Eric rides his bike each week for 10 weeks.

$2\frac{1}{2}$ miles, $2\frac{5}{8}$ miles, $2\frac{3}{4}$ miles, $2\frac{1}{4}$ miles, $2\frac{1}{2}$ miles

$2\frac{1}{2}$ miles, $2\frac{3}{4}$ miles, $2\frac{5}{8}$ miles, $2\frac{5}{8}$ miles, $2\frac{3}{4}$ miles

Create a line plot to represent this data.

(5.MD.B.2)

prepaze

MEASUREMENT & DATA

20. This line plot shows the temperatures recorded in Florida over 12 days.

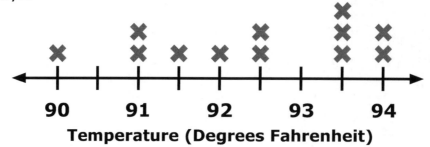

Temperature (Degrees Fahrenheit)

Write 3-4 sentences describing the data represented in this line plot.

_____

_____

_____

_____

5.MD.B.2

UNIT 3:   VOLUME OF SOLID FIGURES

MEASUREMENT & DATA

1. Oliver is filling this box with unit cubes.

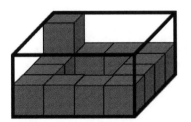

How many more unit cubes does Oliver need to fill this box?

A. 32

B. 19

C. 4

D. 15

5.MD.C.3

2. Joey fills two rectangular prisms with 56 unit cubes.

Both prisms have 4 layers of cubes. The number of cubes in the first layer of the smaller rectangular prism is 6.

What are the volumes of both prisms?

A. 10 cubic units and 46 cubic units

B. 50 cubic units and 6 cubic units

C. 24 cubic units and 32 cubic units

D. 14 cubic units and 42 cubic units

5.MD.C.3

3. Kevin is filling this box with unit cubes.

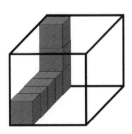

The bottom of the box can be filled with 10 cubes. How many more unit cubes does Kevin need to fill this box?

A. 45   **B.** 8

C. 15   **D.** 38

5.MD.C.3

prepaze

MEASUREMENT & DATA

VOLUME OF SOLID FIGURES

4. The volume of this cube is one cubic unit.

Which solid has a volume of 9 cubic units?

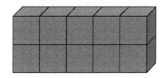

A.

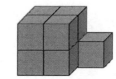

C.

B.

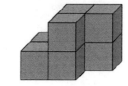

D.

5.MD.C.3

5. The volume of this cube is one cubic unit.

Which solid has a volume equivalent to the 2×3×2 cubic units?

A.

C.

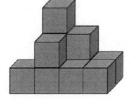

B.

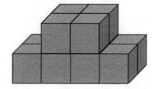

D.

5.MD.C.3

MEASUREMENT & DATA

6. This box is being filled with cubes. Each cube has a volume of 1 cubic unit.

The length of the box is 9 units, and the width of the box is 7 units. What is the volume of this box?

_____

5.MD.C.3

7. This box is being filled with cubes. Each cube has a volume of 1 cubic unit.

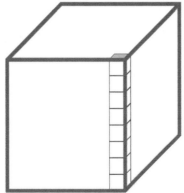

The bottom of the box can be filled with 55 cubes. What is the volume of this box?

_____

5.MD.C.3

MEASUREMENT & DATA

VOLUME OF SOLID FIGURES

8. Which tables show the dimensions of a box that can be filled completely with 720 centimeter cubes?

A.

Length	Width	Height
30 cm	12 cm	2 cm

B.

Length	Width	Height
150 cm	340 cm	230 cm

C.

Length	Width	Height
2 cm	20 cm	6 cm

D.

Length	Width	Height
285 cm	435 cm	105 cm

5.MD.C.4

9. Ava is filling a box with centimeter cubes. The height of the box is 20 centimeters, and he can fit 42 cubes in the base of the box.

How many cubes will fill the box?

A. 2,520   **B.** 120   **C.** 840   **D.** 62

5.MD.C.4

10. Xavier is filling a box with centimeter cubes. The height of the box is 15 centimeters, and he can fill the base of the box with 21 cubes.

How many cubes will fill the box?

A. 36   **B.** 315   **C.** 945   **D.** 72

5.MD.C.4

MEASUREMENT & DATA

11. Josie constructs this solid using one-inch cubes.

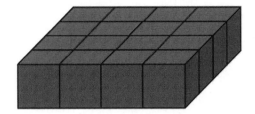

She adds 3 more layers to the solid to create a tower. Each layer has 2 fewer cubes than the layer below it.

What is the volume of the tower?

A. 16 cubic inches

B. 52 cubic inches

C. 64 cubic inches

D. 42 cubic inches

5.MD.C.4

12. Brea constructs this solid using one-inch cubes.

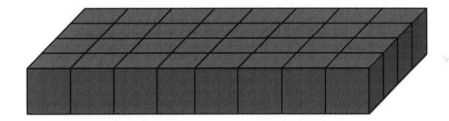

She adds 3 more layers to the solid to create a tower. Each layer has 3 fewer cubes than the layer below it.

What is the volume of the tower?

A. 116 cubic inches   **B.** 128 cubic inches

C. 110 cubic inches   **D.** 32 cubic inches

5.MD.C.4

prepaze

MEASUREMENT & DATA

VOLUME OF SOLID FIGURES

13. Gabriel is measuring a cereal box with centimeter cubes. The box is filled to the halfway point when it has 190 cubes in it. The cereal box has a height of 19 centimeters.

Which picture represents one layer of cubes inside Gabriel's cereal box?

A.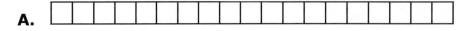

B.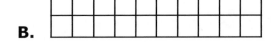

C.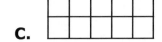

D.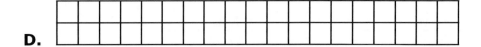

5.MD.C.4

14. Paola is measuring a shipping box with centimeter cubes. The box is filled to the halfway point when it contains 140 cubes. The shipping box has a height of 10 centimeters.

Which picture represents a top view one layer of cubes inside Paola's shipping box?

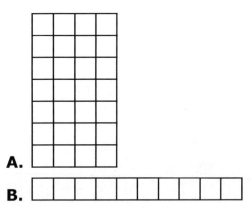

A.

B.

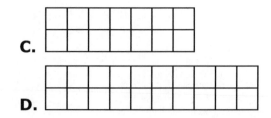

C.

D.

5.MD.C.4

MEASUREMENT & DATA

VOLUME OF SOLID FIGURES

15. Myra wants to fill this box with $\frac{1}{4}$ inch cubes.

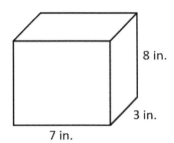

8 in.

3 in.

7 in.

How many cubes are needed to fill this box?

A. 168   **B.** 10,752   **C.** 672   **D.** 2,688

5.MD.C.5

16. Myra fills this box with 1/4 inch cubes.

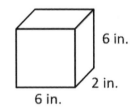

6 in.

2 in.

6 in.

Which statement correctly describes the number of cubes needed to fill this box?

A. There are $(6 \times 4)\,(2 \times 4)$ cubes in one layer.

B. A total of $(6 \times 2 \times 6)$ cubes can fit inside this box.

C. A total of $(24 + 8 + 24)$ cubes can fit inside this box.

D. There are $\frac{1}{4}(6 \times 2)$ cubes in one layer.

5.MD.C.5

prepaze

17. A company packs 128 small boxes inside large crates to be shipped to stores. A picture of the box and crate are shown below.

1.25 ft.

1.25 ft.

1.25 ft.

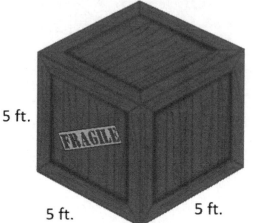

5 ft.

5 ft.

5 ft.

Which expression can be used to find the number of crates needed to ship these boxes?

A. $\left[\left(\frac{5}{1.25}\right)\left(\frac{5}{1.25}\right)\left(\frac{5}{1.25}\right)\right]$

B. $128 + \left[\left(\frac{5}{1.25}\right)\left(\frac{5}{1.25}\right)\left(\frac{5}{1.25}\right)\right]$

C. $\left[\left(\frac{5}{1.25}\right)\left(\frac{5}{1.25}\right)\left(\frac{5}{1.25}\right)\right] - 128$

D. $128 \div \left[\left(\frac{5}{1.25}\right)\left(\frac{5}{1.25}\right)\left(\frac{5}{1.25}\right)\right]$

5.MD.C.5

18. A company packs 500 smaller boxes inside large crates to be shipped to stores.

Each small box is in the shape of a cube and has edge lengths of 0.5 feet. The large crate is also in the shape of a cube and each side as a length of 3 feet

How many crates are needed to ship these boxes?

A. 3   **B.** 2   **C.** 216   **D.** 284

5.MD.C.5

MEASUREMENT & DATA

19. Which prism has the greatest volume?

	Length (in.)	Width (in.)	Height (in.)
Prism A	9	1	1
Prism B	3	1	6
Prism C	4	3	5
Prism D	3	3	3

VOLUME OF SOLID FIGURES

A. Prism A   **B.** Prism B   **C.** Prism C   **D.** Prism D

5.MD.C.5

20. Which prism has the smallest volume?

	Length (in.)	Width (in.)	Height (in.)
Prism A	9	1	1
Prism B	4	1	5
Prism C	4	3	2
Prism D	2	3	3

A. Prism A   **B.** Prism B   **C.** Prism C   **D.** Prism D

5.MD.C.5

CHAPTER REVIEW

prepaze

MEASUREMENT & DATA

1. Paola buys a 5-pound bag of apples. The apples weigh between 5.5 and 5.9 ounces. Approximately how many apples are in the bag?

    A. 100

    B. 7

    C. 10

    D. 14

(5.MD.A.1)

2. Levi buys a 10-pound bag of apples. The apples weigh between 5.1 and 5.4 ounces. Approximately how many apples are in the bag?

    A. 30

    B. 20

    C. 15

    D. 200

(5.MD.A.1)

3. The sign below shows the distance to 2 cities, in the same direction.

| **Dallas** | **27 miles** |
| **Ft. Worth** | **56 miles** |

How many yards are between Dallas and Ft. Worth?

_____

(5.MD.A.1)

4. One time around a race track is 400 meters. How many times do you need to walk around the race track to complete a 5-kilometer race?

_____

(5.MD.A.1)

MEASUREMENT & DATA

5. Dr. Redding uses this line plot to display the amount of growth her patients have had in one year.

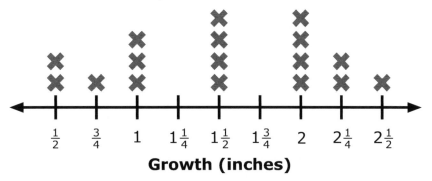

Growth (inches)

Which statement correctly describes information found in this line plot?

A. Dr. Redding has 9 patients.

B. No patient grew $1\frac{1}{4}$ or $1\frac{3}{4}$ inches.

C. The greatest amount of growth is 4 inches.

D. Most patients grew between $\frac{1}{2}$ and 1 inch.

(5.MD.B.2)

6. This line plot shows the daily temperatures in Florida.

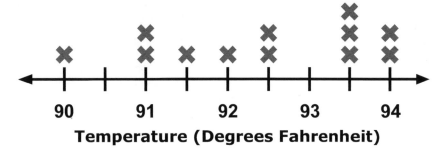

Temperature (Degrees Fahrenheit)

Which statement correctly describes the data on this line plot?

A. The difference between the highest and lowest temperature is 2 degrees.

B. The temperature was 92.25 degrees for 2 days.

C. The temperature ranges from 90 to 94 degrees.

D. The temperature was mostly 93.5 and 94 degrees.

(5.MD.B.2)

prepaze

MEASUREMENT & DATA

7. Liam keeps track of how much paper is recycled by his class each week. The data is shown in this table.

Week	1	2	3	4	5	6	7
Amount of Paper (pounds)	$\frac{3}{4}$	$\frac{5}{8}$	$1\frac{1}{2}$	$\frac{5}{8}$	$\frac{1}{4}$	$1\frac{1}{2}$	$\frac{3}{8}$

Liam plans to use this data to create a line plot. How many data points will be on the line plot?

_____

5.MD.B.2

8. This line plot shows the weight of 12 oranges.

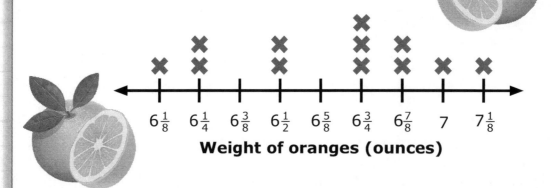

Weight of oranges (ounces)

How many oranges weigh more than $6\frac{4}{8}$ ounces?

_____

5.MD.B.2

MEASUREMENT & DATA

9. Aki uses 64 unit cubes to build one layer of a rectangular prism. The rectangular prism has 9 layers.

How many cubes does Aki use to build the entire rectangular prism?

A. 576 **B.** 146 **C.** 73 **D.** 1,728

(5.MD.C.3)

10. Akio builds a rectangular prism using 324 unit cubes. The rectangular prism has 6 layers.

Which statement correctly describes the rectangular prism Akio builds?

A. The volume of the rectangular prism is 108 cubic units.
B. The length of the rectangular prism is 54 units.
C. The height of the rectangular prism is 108 units.
D. The area of each layer is 54 square units.

(5.MD.C.3)

11. The volume of Paarth's box is 52 cubic units. The box has 4 layers.

How many cubes are in each layer?

A. 48 **B.** 13 **C.** 208 **D.** 56

(5.MD.C.3)

12. The volume of Akio's box is 36 cubic units. The box has 9 layers.

How many cubes are in each layer?

A. 324 **B.** 27 **C.** 45 **D.** 4

(5.MD.C.3)

prepaze

MEASUREMENT & DATA

13. Josie constructs this solid using inch cubes.

She adds 12 more cubes to the solid. What is the new volume of Josie's solid?

_____

5.MD.C.4

14. Hattie constructs this solid using centimeter cubes.

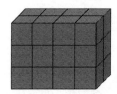

She adds 4 more layers to the solid. What is the new volume of Hattie's solid?

_____

5.MD.C.4

15. The box below has a volume of 280 cubic inches. A stack of cubes is shown in the figure.

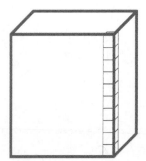

How many cubes are in each of the layers of the box?

_____

5.MD.C.4

MEASUREMENT & DATA

16. Ellen is placing sugar cubes inside this box to measure its height.

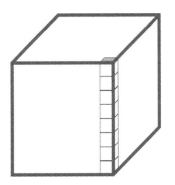

Each sugar cube has a volume of 1 cubic centimeter. The length of the box is equal to 8 sugar cubes, and the width of the box is equal to 6 sugar cubes.

How many sugar cubes can Ellen fit inside this box?

5.MD.C.4

17. What is the volume of the shaded rectangular prism?

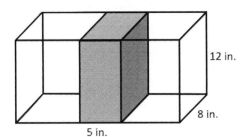

12 in.

8 in.

5 in.

5.MD.C.5

18. The volume of the shaded rectangular prism is $\frac{1}{4}$ the volume of the outer rectangular prism.

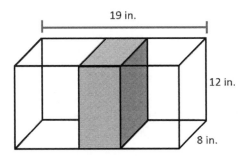

19 in.

12 in.

8 in.

What is the volume of the shaded rectangular prism?

5.MD.C.5

prepaze

MEASUREMENT & DATA

19. Hugo fills this box with $\frac{1}{12}$ foot cubes.

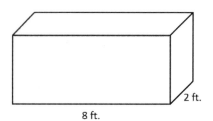

The height of the box is 18 inches. How many $\frac{1}{12}$ foot cubes fit inside this box?

_____

(5.MD.C.5)

20. A company packs smaller boxes inside these large crates to be shipped to stores.

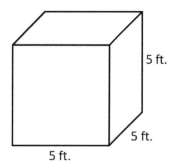

Each small box is in the shape of a cube with edge lengths of 2.5 feet. The company needs to ship 300 small boxes.

How many crates are needed to ship the small boxes?

_____

(5.MD.C.5)

EXTRA PRACTICE

MEASUREMENT & DATA

1. This table shows the distance 4 students live from school.

Student	Distance (feet)
Avi	18,216
Fredo	7,656
Gabriel	3,802
Haley	10,454

The school bus will pick up any student who lives more than 1.5 miles from school. How would you determine which of these students are able to ride the bus to school?

_____

_____

_____

5.MD.A.1

2. This table shows the elevation of 4 mountains

Mountain	Elevation (meters above sea level)
Kubi Gangri	6,859
Makalu	8,485
Antaleo	3,264
Distaghil Sar	7,885

Which mountains have an elevation greater than 5 kilometers? Explain your reasoning.

_____

_____

_____

5.MD.A.1

prepaze

MEASUREMENT & DATA

3. Gan and Ian are measuring the height of a bookshelf. The bookshelf is 6 feet tall. Gan says the height of the bookshelf is 72 inches. Ian says the height of the bookshelf is 3 yards. Do you agree with Gan and Ian? Explain your reasoning.

_____

_____

_____

_____

5.MD.A.1

4. Jada and Diego are measuring the amount of time it takes for their class to walk from the music room to the lunch room.

It takes 6 minutes to walk from the music room to the lunch room.

Jada says it takes 360 seconds to walk to the lunch room. Diego says it takes $\frac{1}{12}$ hour to walk to the lunch room.

Do you agree with Jada and Diego? Explain your reasoning.

_____

_____

_____

_____

5.MD.A.1

prepaze

MEASUREMENT & DATA

5. This line plot displays the length of some leaves Yaminah collected.

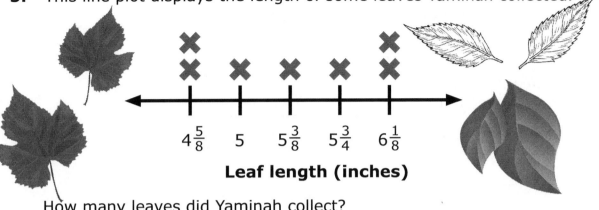

Leaf length (inches)

How many leaves did Yaminah collect?

A. 5 **B.** 7 **C.** 6 **D.** 4

5.MD.B.2

6. This line plot displays the amount of juice consumed by the students in a class.

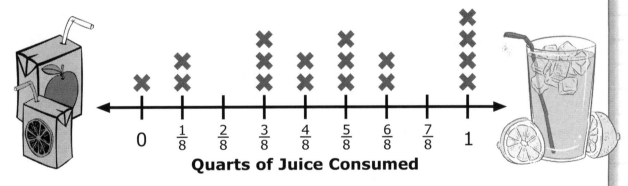

Quarts of Juice Consumed

Write 3-4 sentences describing the data represented in this line plot.

_____

_____

_____

5.MD.B.2

prepaze

7. Lily keeps track of how much paper is recycled by his class each week. The data is shown in this table.

Week	1	2	3	4	5	6	7
Amount of Paper (pounds)	$\frac{3}{8}$	$\frac{7}{8}$	1	$\frac{1}{2}$	$\frac{7}{8}$	1	$\frac{3}{8}$

Create a line plot using the data in this table.

5.MD.B.2

8. This line plot shows the weight of 12 oranges.

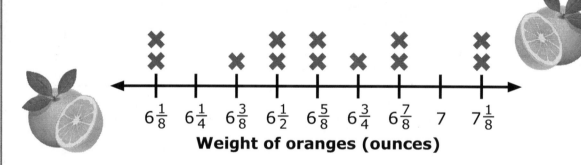

Weight of oranges (ounces)

How would you determine the difference between the heaviest and the lightest orange?

_____

_____

_____

5.MD.B.2

MEASUREMENT & DATA

9. Asha puts 8 layers of unit cubes inside a box and it is one-third full. There are 41 cubes in each layer.

How many more cubes does Asha need to fill the box?

A. 984   **B.** 656   **C.** 596   **D.** 123

5.MD.C.3

10. Avi places 154 cubes inside a box and it is $\frac{2}{3}$ full. The width of the box is 11 units and the length of the box is 7 units.

What is the height of the box?

A. 77 units   **B.** 231 units   **C.** 2 units   **D.** 3 units

5.MD.C.3

11. Alan builds a rectangular prism using unit cubes. One layer of the prism is made up of 28 units cubes, and there is a total of 10 layers.

What is the volume of the prism Alan builds?

_____

5.MD.C.3

12. The volume of the shaded prism is $\frac{1}{4}$ the volume of the prism surrounding it.

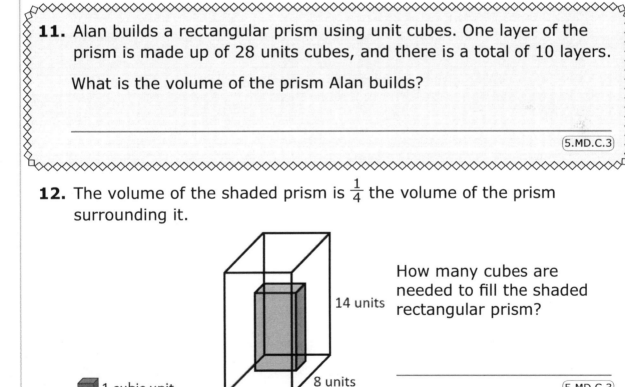

14 units

How many cubes are needed to fill the shaded rectangular prism?

1 cubic unit

8 units

5 units

_____

5.MD.C.3

prepaze

MEASUREMENT & DATA

13. Anvi is putting caramel candies in four boxes. Each candy is in the shape of a cube which is 1 centimeter long on each edge.

Two of the boxes are 3 centimeters long on each edge.

Two of the boxes have a height of 4 centimeters, and the bottom of the box can be filled with 10 candies.

How many caramel candies will fit inside the four boxes?

A. 67   **B.** 54   **C.** 80   **D.** 134

5.MD.C.4

14. Ami is putting caramel candies in two boxes. Each candy is in the shape of a cube which is 1 centimeter long on each edge.

Each box is 8 centimeters long and 7 centimeters high. The width of the box is half of the length.

How many caramel candies can Ami fit inside two boxes?

A. 224   **B.** 448   **C.** 196   **D.** 392

5.MD.C.4

15. Which solid has the greatest volume?

Solid A	Solid B	Solid C	Solid D

A. Solid A

B. Solid B

C. Solid C

D. Solid D

5.MD.C.4

MEASUREMENT & DATA

16. Joey builds a rectangular prism using 1-inch cubes. He removes 8 cubes from the interior of this prism to create this figure.

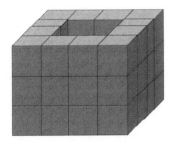

What is the volume of the figure?

A. 8 cubic inches

B. 12 cubic inches

C. 40 cubic inches

D. 48 cubic inches

5.MD.C.4

17. A swimming pool is 6 feet deep, 12 feet long, and 8 feet wide. How much water is needed to fill $\frac{3}{4}$ of the pool?

A. 432 cubic feet   **B.** 576 cubic feet

C. 144 cubic feet   **D.** 288 cubic feet

5.MD.C.5

18. A swimming pool is 4 feet deep, 10 feet long, and 12 feet wide. Which equation can be used to determine how much water, x, is needed to fill $\frac{3}{8}$ of this swimming pool?

A. $\frac{3}{8}(4 + 10 + 12) = x$

B. $\frac{8(4+10+12)}{3} = x$

C. $\frac{3}{8}(4 \times 10 \times 12) = x$

D. $\frac{8(4 \times 10 \times 12)}{3} = x$

5.MD.C.5

MEASUREMENT & DATA

EXTRA PRACTICE

19. A cube has a dimension of 12 centimeters. A rectangular prism has a width of 6 centimeters, a length of 4 centimeters, and a height of 2 centimeters. Which solid has the greater volume? Explain your reasoning.

_____

_____

_____

5.MD.C.5

20. Which has a greater volume: a cube with a volume of 1 cubic foot, or a cube with edge lengths of 11 inches? Explain why.

_____

_____

_____

5.MD.C.5

GEOMETRY

prepaze

www.prepaze.com

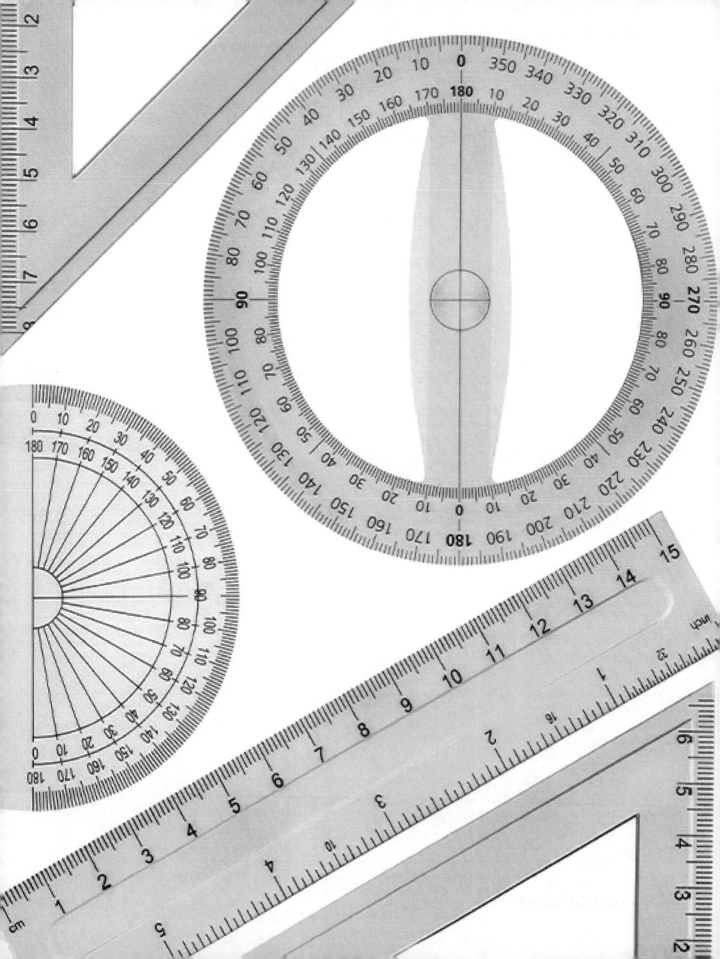

GEOMETRY

1. What is the x-coordinate of Point *D*?

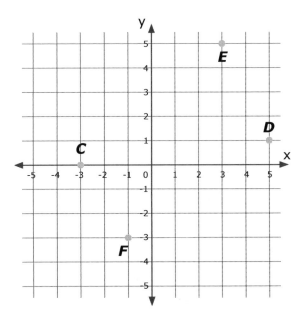

A. 1

B. 5

C. -5

D. -1

5.G.A.1

2. What is the y-coordinate of the Point *F*?

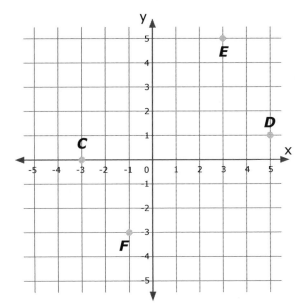

A. -1

B. 3

C. 1

D. -3

5.G.A.1

prepaze

GEOMETRY

GRAPHING AND COORDINATE PLANES

3. What is the x-coordinate of the Point *E*?

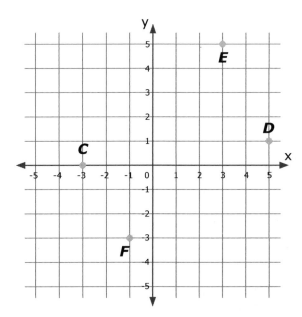

A. 5

B. -5

C. 3

D. -3

5.G.A.1

4. What is the y-coordinate of Point *C*?

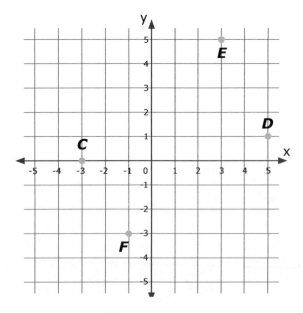

A. 0

B. -4

C. 3

D. -3

5.G.A.1

GEOMETRY

5. Which ordered pair represents Point *H*?

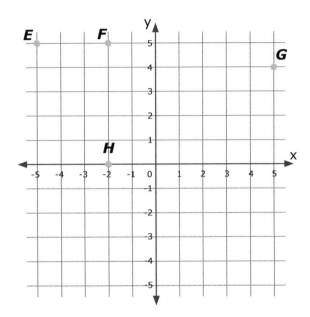

A. (-2, 0)

B. (2, 0)

C. (0, -2)

D. (0, 2)

5.G.A.1

6. Which ordered pair represents Point *E*?

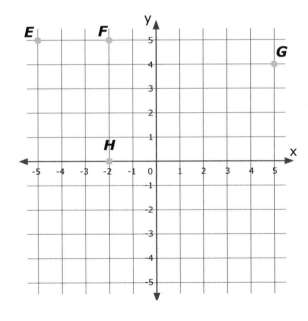

A. (5, -5)

B. (-5, 5)

C. (-5, 0)

D. (0, -5)

5.G.A.1

prepaze

GEOMETRY

GRAPHING AND COORDINATE PLANES

7.   **True or False:** The ordered pair representing Point *P* is (-5, 2).

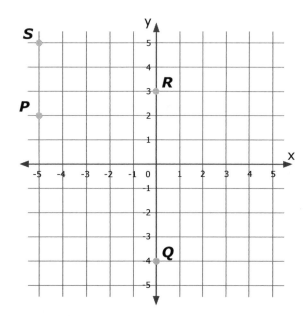

A. True

B. False

5.G.A.1

8.   **True or False:** The ordered pair representing Point *Q* is (0, -4).

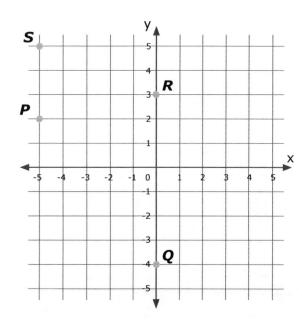

A. True

B. False

5.G.A.1

GEOMETRY

9. **True or False:** The ordered pair representing Point *S* is (5, -5).

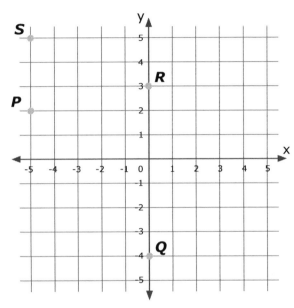

A. True

B. False

5.G.A.1

10. True or False: The ordered pair representing Point *R* is (0, 3).

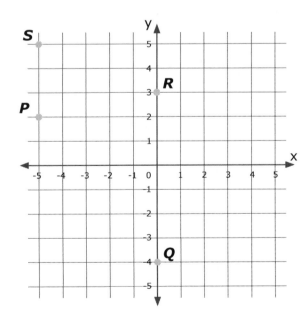

A. True

B. False

5.G.A.1

prepaze

GEOMETRY

11. The ordered pair representing Point *Q* is _____.

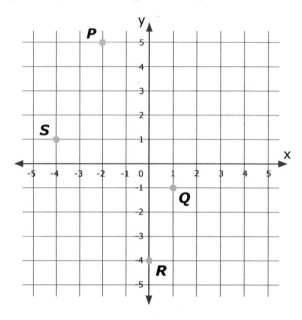

5.G.A.1

12. The ordered pair representing Point *S* is _____.

5.G.A.1

GEOMETRY

13. The ordered pair representing Point *P* is _____.

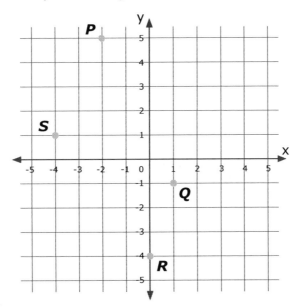

5.G.A.1

14. The ordered pair representing Point *R* is _____.

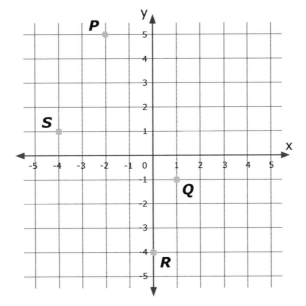

5.G.A.1

GRAPHING AND
COORDINATE PLANES

prepaze

GEOMETRY

15. The ordered pair representing Point *T* is _____.

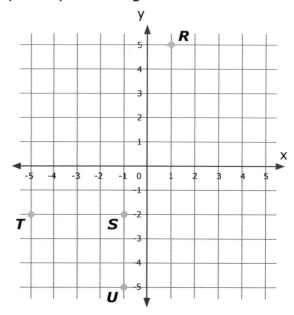

5.G.A.1

16. The ordered pair representing Point *U* is _____.

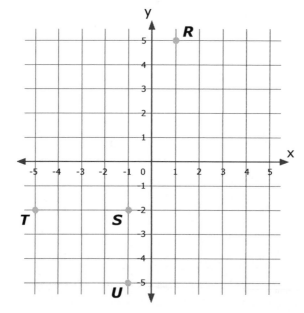

5.G.A.1

GEOMETRY

17. The ordered pair representing Point *R* is _____.

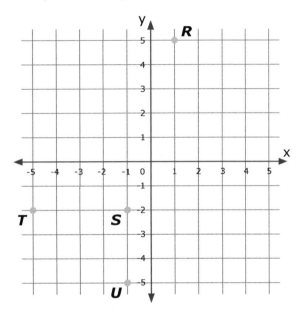

18. The ordered pair representing Point *S* is _____.

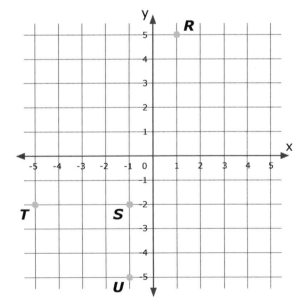

GRAPHING AND
COORDINATE PLANES

prepaze

GEOMETRY

19. The ordered pair representing Point *T* is _____.

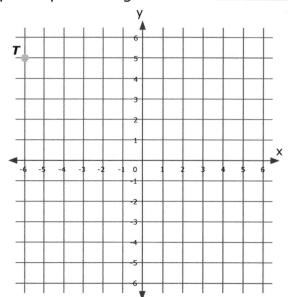

(5.G.A.1)

20. The ordered pair representing Point *U* is _____.

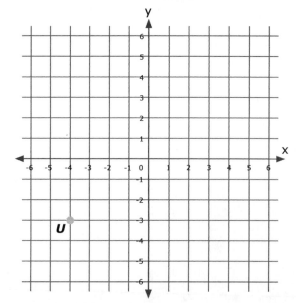

(5.G.A.1)

UNIT 2:   PROBLEM SOLVING USING GRAPHING

GEOMETRY

1. What are the coordinates of point R?

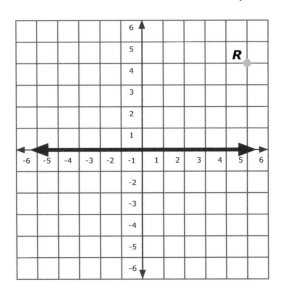

A. (5,-5)

B. (5,4)

C. (-4,5)

D. (5,3)

5.G.A.2

2. What are the coordinates of point A?

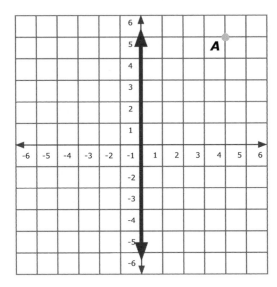

A. (4,5)

B. (5,4)

C. (5,5)

D. (3,5)

5.G.A.2

prepaze

GEOMETRY

PROBLEM SOLVING USING GRAPHING

3. What are the coordinates of point T?

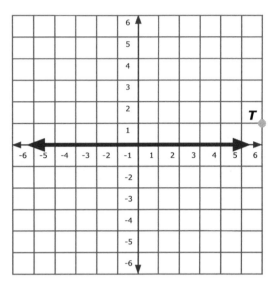

A. (5,1)

B. (6,4)

C. (6,1)

D. (5,2)

5.G.A.2

4. At which point is the restaurant located on this graph?

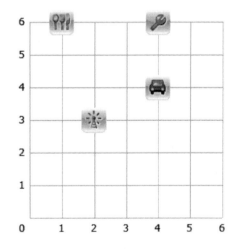

car dealership

radio tower

hardware store

restaurant

A. (2,3)

B. (4,4)

C. (6,4)

D. (1,6)

5.G.A.2

GEOMETRY

5. At which point is the car dealership located on this graph?

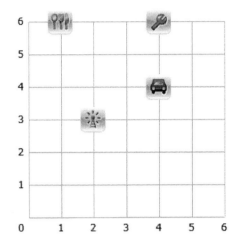

🚗 car dealership	**A.** (2,3)	
📡 radio tower	**B.** (4,4)	
🔧 hardware store	**C.** (6,4)	
🍴 restaurant	**D.** (1,6)	

5.G.A.2

6. At which point is the radio tower located on this graph?

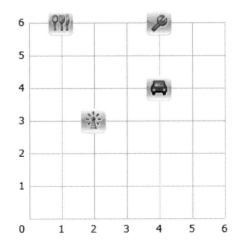

🚗 car dealership	**A.** (2,3)	
📡 radio tower	**B.** (4,4)	
🔧 hardware store	**C.** (6,4)	
🍴 restaurant	**D.** (1,6)	

5.G.A.2

prepaze

NAME: _____ DATE: _____

GEOMETRY

PROBLEM SOLVING USING GRAPHING

7. Where is the hardware store located on this graph?

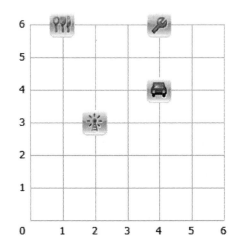

car dealership	**A.**	(2,3)
radio tower	**B.**	(4,4)
hardware store	**C.**	(6,4)
restaurant	**D.**	(4,6)

5.G.A.2

8. What is located at (2, 4)?

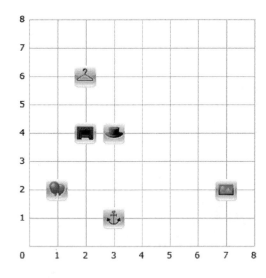

A. Party Supply Store

B. Dry cleaners

C. Harbor

D. Theater

5.G.A.2

GEOMETRY

9. What is located at (3, 1)?

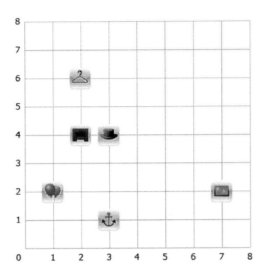

A. Party Supply Store

B. Dry Cleaners

C. Harbor

D. Magic Shop

5.G.A.2

10. What is located at (2, 6)?

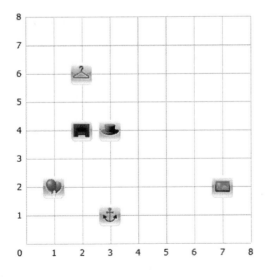

A. Party Supply Store

B. Dry Cleaners

C. Harbor

D. Magic Shop

5.G.A.2

prepaze

GEOMETRY

11. You start at (2,5) which is where the post office is located and you need to get to the grocery store. You move left 1 unit to get to the grocery store. At which point is the grocery store?

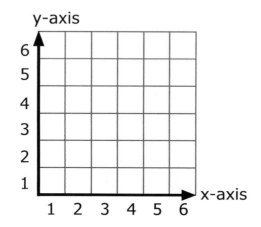

5.G.A.2

12. You start at the park which is at the coordinates (2,3). You move right 3 units to get to the ball field. At which point is the ball field?

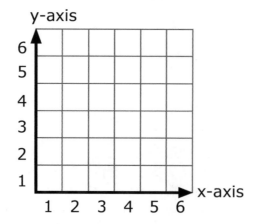

5.G.A.2

GEOMETRY

13. You start at (4,3) which are the coordinates for your house, and you want to get to the outside storage building to get your bike. You move up 1 unit. What are the coordinates of the outside storage building?

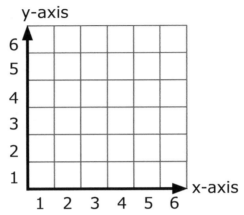

5.G.A.2

14. You start at your friend's house which has the coordinates (5,3). You move down 2 units to get to the sidewalk. At which point do you reach the sidewalk?

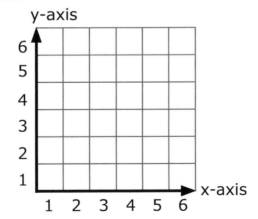

5.G.A.2

prepaze

GEOMETRY

15. Your mother started at (2,4) which are the coordinates of the shopping center. She has to move up 1 unit to get to her car. At which point is the car?

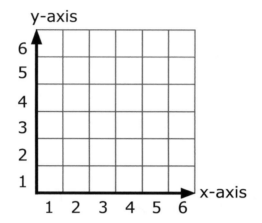

5.G.A.2

16. Houston starts at the coordinates of (1,4) and to get to the baseball diamond, he moves up 2 units. At which point is the baseball diamod?

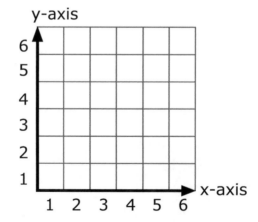

5.G.A.2

GEOMETRY

17. Lindsay starts at (6,5), the coordinates for her favorite toy store. She moves down 1 unit to get to the ice cream parlor. At which point is the ice cream parlor?

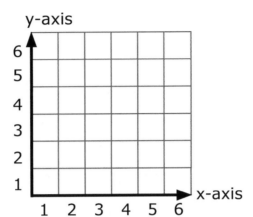

5.G.A.2

18. Place a point on the coordinates (4,2) which is where the school is located.

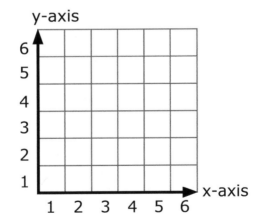

5.G.A.2

prepaze

GEOMETRY

19. Place a point on the coordinates (5,5) which represent the location of a football field.

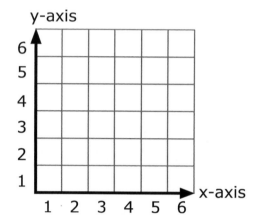

5.G.A.2

20. Place a point on the coordinates (0,4) which represents where your best friend lives.

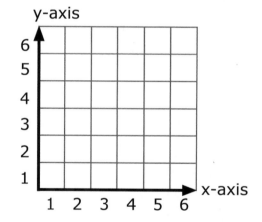

5.G.A.2

UNIT 3:   CLASSIFICATION OF SHAPES

GEOMETRY

1. What name best describes this shape?

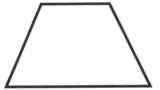

- **A.** Square
- **B.** Kite
- **C.** Triangle
- **D.** Quadrilateral

5.G.B.3

2. How many right angles does this quadrilateral have?

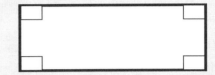

- **A.** 2
- **B.** 4
- **C.** 6
- **D.** 5

5.G.B.3

3. What name best describes this shape?

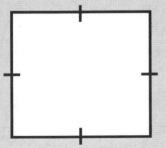

- **A.** Parallelogram
- **B.** Trapezoid
- **C.** Square
- **D.** Triangle

5.G.B.3

4. What name best describes this shape?

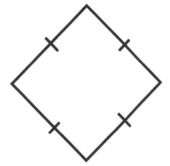

- **A.** Quadrilateral
- **B.** Parallelogram
- **C.** Rhombus
- **D.** Triangle

5.G.B.3

prepaze

GEOMETRY

5. What name best describes this shape?

A. Square

B. Triangle

C. Rectangle

D. Parallelogram

5.G.B.3

6. **True or False:** The name best that describes this shape is a quadrilateral.

A. True   **B.** False

5.G.B.3

7. **True or False:** The name that best describes this shape is a rhombus.

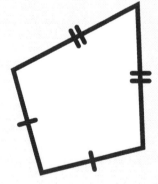

A. True   **B.** False

5.G.B.3

8. **True or False:** The name that best describes this shape is quadrilateral.

A. True   **B.** False

5.G.B.3

GEOMETRY

9. **True or False:** The name that best describes this shape is the rhombus.

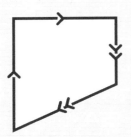

A. True   **B.** False

(5.G.B.3)

10. **True or False:** Two pairs of opposite sides in the figure below are parallel.

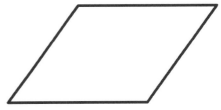

A. True   **B.** False

(5.G.B.3)

11. **True or False:** A nonagon has 9 sides.

A. True   **B.** False

(5.G.B.4)

12. **True or False:** A heptagon has 8 sides.

A. True   **B.** False

(5.G.B.4)

13. **True or False:** This shape is a polygon.

A. True   **B.** False

(5.G.B.4)

14. **True or False:** An octagon has 5 sides.

A. True   **B.** False

(5.G.B.4)

15. **True or False:** This shape is a regular polygon.

A. True

B. False

(5.G.B.4)

prepaze

GEOMETRY

16. What name best describes this shape?

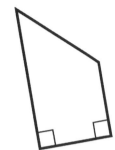

5.G.B.4

17. What name best describes this shape?

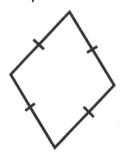

5.G.B.4

18. What name best describes this shape?

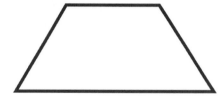

5.G.B.4

19. What name best describes this shape?

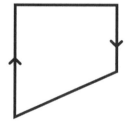

5.G.B.4

20. What name best describes this shape?

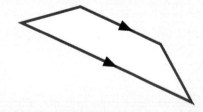

5.G.B.4

CHAPTER REVIEW

GEOMETRY

1. Which ordered pair represents Point *G*?

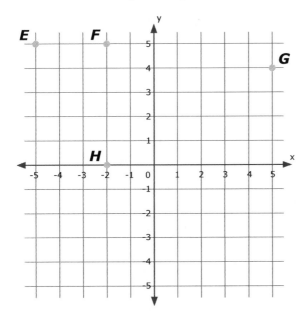

A. (4, 5)

B. (5, 0)

C. (4, 4)

D. (5, 4)

5.G.A.1

2. What are the coordinates of point *F*?

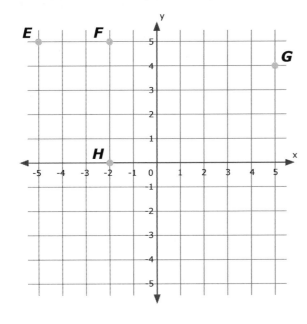

A. (5, -2)

B. (0, 5)

C. (-2, 5)

D. (5, 2)

5.G.A.1

prepaze

GEOMETRY

3. Create a point on the graph to represent the coordinates (4, 2)

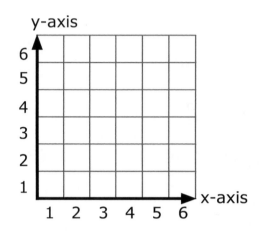

5.G.A.1

4. Create a point on the graph to represents the coordinates (2, 5)

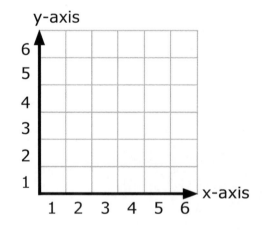

5.G.A.1

prepaze

GEOMETRY

5. What is located at the coordinates (1,2)?

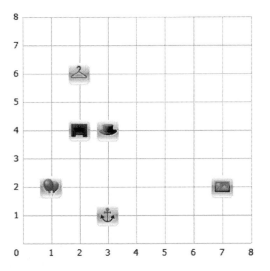

A. Party Supply Store

B. Dry Cleaners

C. Harbor

D. Magic Shop

(5.G.A.2)

6. What is located at the coordinates (7,2)?

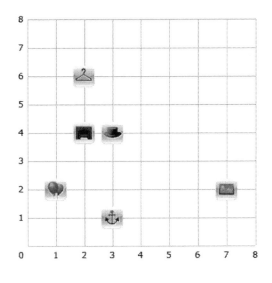

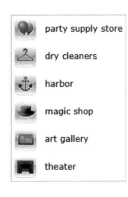

A. Party Supply Store

B. Dry Cleaners

C. Harbor

D. Art Gallery

(5.G.A.2)

prepaze

GEOMETRY

7. What is located at the coordinates (3,4)?

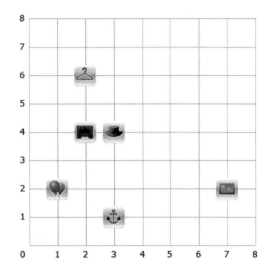

A. Party Supply Store

B. Dry Cleaners

C. Harbor

D. Magic Shop

5.G.A.2

8. Plot a point at the coordinates (3,6) on this graph.

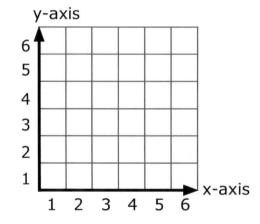

5.vG.A.2

GEOMETRY

9. What name best describes this shape?

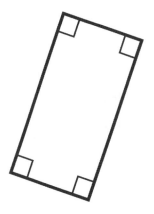

    A. Square

    B. B Rhombus

    C. Rectangle

    D. Triangle

5.G.B.3

10. What name best describes this shape?

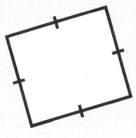

    A. Square

    B. B Rhombus

    C. Rectangle

    D. Parallelogram

5.G.B.3

11. What name best describes this shape?

    A. Rhombus

    B. Trapezoid

    C. Square

    D. Quadrilateral

5.G.B.3

prepaze

GEOMETRY

12. What name best describes this shape?

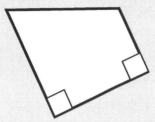

A. Rhombus
B. Trapezoid
C. Quadrilateral
D. Square

5.G.B.3

13. True or False: Two pairs of opposite sides are parallel.

A. True
B. False

5.G.B.3

14. True or False: The name that best describes this shape is the rectangle.

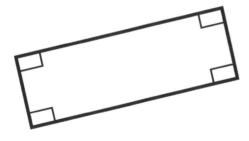

A. True
B. False

5.G.B.3

15. True or False: A hexagon has 3 sides.

A. True   **B.** False

5.G.B.4

16. True or False: A quadrilateral has 4 sides.

A. True   **B.** False

5.G.B.4

prep@ze

GEOMETRY

17. True or False: This shape is a regular polygon.

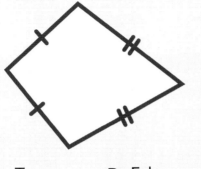

A. True   **B.** False

5.G.B.4

18. True or False: This shape is a regular polygon.

A. True   **B.** False

5.G.B.4

19. True or False: This triangle is a scalene triangle.

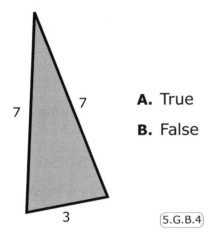

A. True

B. False

5.G.B.4

20. A triangle has side lengths of 5 meters, 11 meters, and 11 meters. This triangle is an isosceles triangle.

A. True   **B.** False

5.G.B.4

EXTRA PRACTICE

GEOMETRY

1. What is the ordered pair represented by Point *R*? _____.

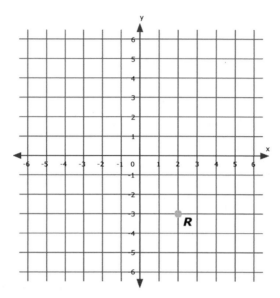

5.G.A.1

2. What is the ordered pair represented by Point *S*? _____.

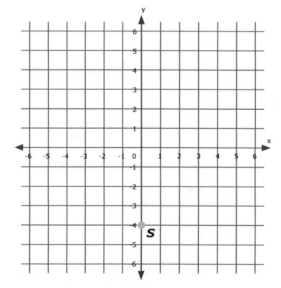

5.G.A.1

GEOMETRY

3. Which point on the graph below is located at the coordinates (3, 3)?

_____

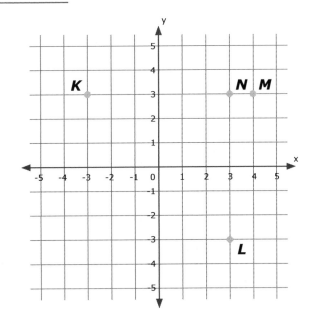

5.G.A.1

4. Graph the point (6, 3) on the coordinate plane below.

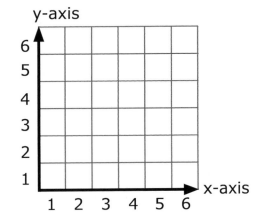

5.G.A.1

prepaze

GEOMETRY

5. This coordinate graph shows the location of Sue's house. The movie theater is located 2 blocks east and 4 blocks south of Sue's house. What ordered pair would represent the location of the movie theater?

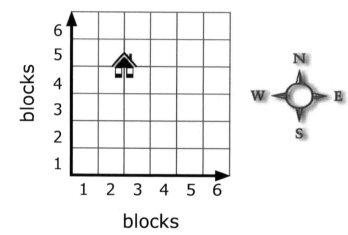

blocks

5.G.A.2

6. Alana is drawing a heart on this coordinate grid 2 units above and 3 units to the right of star.

What ordered pair represents the location of the heart?

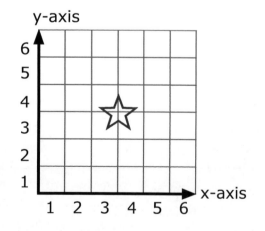

5.G.A.2

GEOMETRY

7. Enrique wants to draw a square 2 units to the left and 1 unit below the diamond. What ordered pair represents the location of the square?

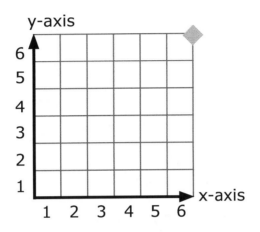

5.G.A.2

8. Siri plans to draw a triangle 4 units to the right and 4 units above the heart. What ordered pair represents the location of the triangle?

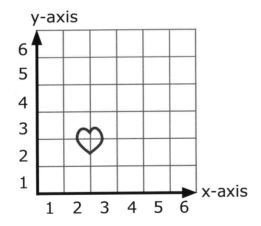

5.G.A.2

prepaze

GEOMETRY

9. **True or False:** The name that best describes this shape is a rhombus.

A. True   **B.** False

5.G.B.3

10. **True or False:** The name that best describes this shape is the square.

A. True   **B.** False

5.G.B.3

11. **True or False:** This quadrilateral is a trapezoid.

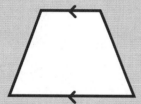

A. True   **B.** False

5.G.B.3

12. **True or False:** This quadrilateral is a trapezoid.

A. True   **B.** False

5.G.B.3

13. **True or False:** This quadrilateral is a parallelogram.

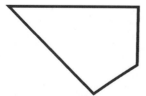

A. True   **B.** False

5.G.B.3

14. **True or False:** This quadrilateral is a trapezoid.

A. True   **B.** False

5.G.B.3

GEOMETRY

15. True or False: This triangle is an isosceles triangle.

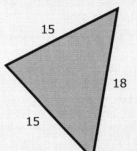

15
18
15

A. True   **B.** False

5.G.B.4

16. True or False: A triangle has angle measurements of 32°, 115°, and 33°.

True or False: The triangle is a right triangle.

A. True

B. False

5.G.B.4

EXTRA PRACTICE

17. True or False: This is a scalene triangle.

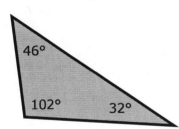

46°
102°   32°

A. True   **B.** False

5.G.B.4

18. True or False: This triangle is an equilateral triangle.

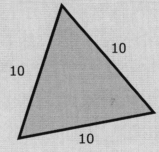

10
10
10

A. True   **B.** False

5.G.B.4

19. True or False: This triangle is an obtuse triangle.

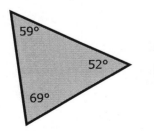

59°
52°
69°

A. True

B. False

5.G.B.4

20. True or False: A scalene triangle has three equal sides.

A. True   **B.** False

5.G.B.4

prepaze

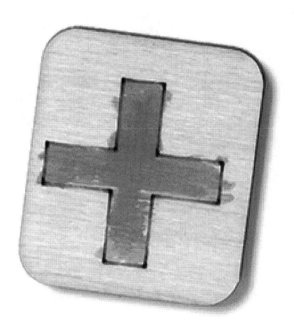

COMPREHENSIVE ASSESSMENTS

ASSESSMENT ①

COMPREHENSIVE ASSESSMENTS

1. When simplifying this expression, what step should you take first?

$$8 \times 4 + \{2 \times [24 - (8 + 4)]\}$$

A. Subtract 8 from 24

B. Multiply 2 and 24

C. Multiply 8 and 4

D. Add 8 and 4

(5.OA.A.1)

2. The value of Expression A will be _____7_____ times the sum of 1,684 and 267.

1951

Expression A: $(3 + 4)(267 + 1,684)$

7   1951

$\begin{array}{r} 1684 \\ + 267 \\ \hline 1951 \end{array}$

(5.OA.A.2)

3. **True or False:** In this table, when the x-value is 10, the corresponding y-value will be 16.

x	2	4	6
y	3	6	9

8   10
12   15

A. True   **B.** False

(5.OA.B.3)

4. The rule for finding a sequence of numbers on a graph is "x is half of y".

True or False: When the y-value is 40, the x-value is 20.

A. True   **B.** False $x = y \times \frac{1}{2}$

(5.OA.B.3)

5. Using the number 7.251, fill in the blanks below.

A. Ones digit: _____7_____

B. Tenths digit: _____2_____

C. Hundredths digit: _____5_____

D. Thousandths digit: _____1_____

(5.NBT.A.1)

ASSESSMENT ①

prepaze

COMPREHENSIVE ASSESSMENTS

ASSESSMENT 1

6. Write in the value of each digit in the number 34.827.

2: _hundreths_

3: _tens_

7: _thousandths_

4: _ones_

8: _tenths_

5.NBT.A.1

7. What is the standard notation of 7.82×10^2?

A. 78.2

B. 782

C. 7,820

D. 78,200

5.NBT.A.2

8. Solve:
$12.4 \times 10^3 =$ ___ D ___

_10,000_

A. 124

B. 1,240

C. 12,400

D. 124,000

5.NBT.A.2

9. Write this number in standard form.

$$5 \times 10 + 8 \times 1 + 2 \times (1/10) + 1 \times (1/100) + 3 \times (1/1,000)$$

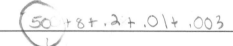

_50 + 8 + .2 + .01 + .003_

5.NBT.A.3

10. Write this number in standard form.

$$6 \times 100 + 7 \times 10 + 9 \times 1 + 1 \times (1/10) + 2 \times (1/100) + 8 \times (1/1,000)$$

_600 + 70 + 9 + .1 + .02 + .008_

5.NBT.A.3

prepaze

COMPREHENSIVE ASSESSMENTS

ASSESSMENT ①

11. A question on Al's test required him to round 2.3482 to a specific decimal place. Which response would NOT be a correct answer?

A. 2.4   **B.** 2.3

C. 2.35   **D.** 2.0

(5.NBT.A.4)

12. There are 392 fifth graders entering middle school next year, all traveling to school by bus. If each bus can carry 48 students, how many buses are required to go to the middle school for a visit?

6
48
× 8
384

A. 6   **B.** 7

C. 8   **D.** 9

48 ⟌392

(5.NBT.A.4)

13. Workers in a factory earn $9/hour. They work 40 hours every week. If there are 138 workers, how much does the company pay every week in wages?

A. $39,744   **B.** $52,164

C. $49,680   **D.** $52,668

(5.NBT.B.5)

14. An art gallery sells 15 paintings in 1 day. If the average price is $1024, how much money did the gallery make that day?

A. $15,630   **B.** $10,280

C. $12,630   **D.** $15,360

(5.NBT.B.5)

15. John is giving his sisters gift bags with candy. He has 5 bags of one type of candy and 10 bags of another type of candy. If he has three sisters, how many bags of candy will each sister receive?

A. 2   **B.** 3   **C.** 4   **D.** 5

(5.NBT.B.6)

16. Alison is making necklaces with beads. If she has 267 beads and each necklace takes 30 beads, how many beads will she have left over?

A. 8   **B.** 9   **C.** 24   **D.** 27

$30\overline{)267}$
240
027

(5.NBT.B.6)

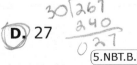

COMPREHENSIVE ASSESSMENTS

ASSESSMENT 1

17. Joseph drove his truck for $2\frac{1}{2}$ hours at a speed of 63 miles per hour. How far did he drive? $126 + 31.5$

A. 126 miles

B. 157.5 miles

C. 189 miles

D. 25.2 miles

5.NBT.B.7

18. Emily joined a gym that costs $39.89 a month. About how much will she pay for her gym membership per year?

A. $80   B. $40

C. $480   D. $360

5.NBT.B.7

19. A recipe required $\frac{3}{5}$ cups of white sugar and $\frac{1}{4}$ cups of brown sugar. When the two sugars were combined, how much sugar was used altogether? $\frac{3}{5} + \frac{1}{4}$

A. $\frac{4}{5}$ cups   B. $\frac{2}{9}$ cups

C. $\frac{13}{20}$ cups   D. $\frac{17}{20}$ cups

$\frac{12}{20} + \frac{5}{20}$

5.NF.A.1

20. Olivia was reading two books at the same time. She read $\frac{7}{8}$ of the first book, and $\frac{1}{6}$ of the second book. What combined fraction of both books did she read?

A. $\frac{8}{48}$ B. $\frac{46}{48}$

C. $\frac{50}{48}$ D. $\frac{48}{50}$

$\frac{1}{6} + \frac{7}{8}$

5.NF.A.1

21. A baker is making an apple pie. She needs $\frac{2}{5}$ teaspoons of cinnamon and $\frac{1}{3}$ teaspoons of nutmeg. When the two spices are combined, how much spice is used altogether?

A. $\frac{10}{15}$ teaspoons   B. $\frac{11}{15}$ teaspoons

C. $\frac{12}{15}$ teaspoons   D. $\frac{13}{15}$ teaspoons

5.NF.A.2

prepaze   www.prepaze.com

COMPREHENSIVE ASSESSMENTS

22. A can of paint was $\frac{4}{5}$ full. Alex used $\frac{2}{3}$ of the remaining paint. What expression can be used to determine the fraction of the paint left in the can?

A. $\frac{4}{5} + \frac{4}{5}$ **B.** $\frac{4}{5} - \frac{2}{3}$ **C.** $\frac{4}{5} + \frac{2}{3}$ **D.** $\frac{2}{3} - \frac{4}{5}$

(5.NF.A.2)

23. A fraction of the figure below is shaded. Which expression represents this fraction as a division problem?

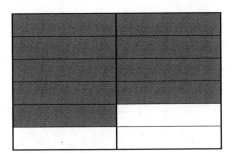

A. 9×12

B. $9 \div 12$

C. 3×12

D. $3 \div 12$

(5.NF.B.3)

24. Which response represents $4 \div 5$ as a fraction?

 Start here!

A. $\frac{4}{20}$ **B.** $\frac{5}{4}$ **C.** $\frac{4}{5}$ **D.** $\frac{4}{9}$

(5.NF.B.3)

25. Simplify: $4 \times \frac{2}{3}$

A. $\frac{8}{3}$ **B.** $\frac{6}{3}$ **C.** $\frac{2}{3}$ **D.** $\frac{14}{3}$

(5.NF.B.4)

26. Solve: $3 \times \frac{4}{5}$

A. $\frac{7}{5}$ **B.** $\frac{15}{4}$ **C.** $\frac{19}{5}$ **D.** $\frac{12}{5}$

(5.NF.B.4)

prepaze

COMPREHENSIVE ASSESSMENTS

27. A can of paint was $\frac{3}{4}$ full. Tori used $\frac{4}{5}$ of the remaining paint, what fraction of the entire can of paint did Tori use?

A. $\frac{12}{20}$ of the entire can of paint   **B.** $\frac{6}{10}$ of the entire can of paint

C. $\frac{3}{5}$ of the entire can of paint   **D.** All of the above.

5.NF.B.5

28. Kelly used $1\frac{1}{3}$ teaspoons of cinnamon for each batch of French toast in a restaurant. If she made 21 batches of French toast, how many teaspoons of cinnamon did Kelly use in all?

A. 26   **B.** 27   **C.** 28   **D.** 29

$$\frac{21}{1} \times \frac{4}{3} = \frac{84}{3}$$

$$3\overline{)84}$$ 28

5.NF.B.5

29. Chris spent $2\frac{1}{8}$ hours on math homework every day for $5\frac{2}{5}$ days. How many hours did Chris spend on his math homework?

A. $11\frac{3}{8}$ **B.** $11\frac{7}{8}$ **C.** $11\frac{19}{40}$ **D.** $11\frac{1}{4}$

$$\frac{17}{8} \times \frac{27}{5} = \frac{459}{40} = 11.475$$

5.NF.B.6

30. Travis earns $\$15$ a week from completing his chores. How much money does Travis earn in $6\frac{1}{10}$ weeks?

$$\frac{61}{10} \times \frac{15}{1} = \frac{915}{10}$$

A. $\$91$ **B.** $\$91.50$ **C.** $\$92$ **D.** $\$92.50$

5.NF.B.6

31. Simplify: $7 \div \frac{7}{8}$. $\frac{56}{7}$

8

5.NF.B.7

COMPREHENSIVE ASSESSMENTS

32. This table shows the weight of 4 containers of berries.

Fruit	Weight (pounds)
Strawberries	1.55
Blackberries	1.38
Raspberries	1.2
Blueberries	1.39

Edward estimates the 4 containers weigh a total of 64 ounces. Do you agree with Edward? Explain your reasoning.

no this estimate is too

below

(5.MD.A.1)

33. This line plot shows the weight of 8 oranges.

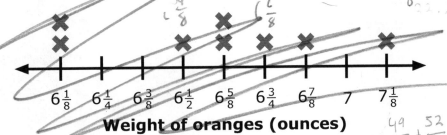

Weight of oranges (ounces)

What is the combined weight, in ounces, of the oranges?

39.875   52.15

(5.MD.B.2)

34. Dev uses a layer of 99 cubes to fill the base of this rectangular prism.

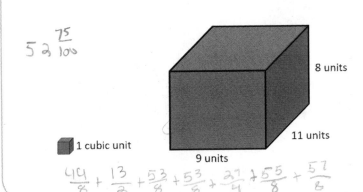

1 cubic unit

9 units

11 units

8 units

How many layers of 99 cubes does Dev need to fill the rectangular prism?

A. 9   **B.** 8
C. 11   **D.** 3

(5.MD.C.3)

prepaze

COMPREHENSIVE ASSESSMENTS

ASSESSMENT 1

35. Hyun uses 80 cubes to fill the base of this rectangular prism.

16 units

1 cubic unit

7 units

5 units

How many layers of 80 cubes does Hyun need to fill this rectangular prism?

A. 16   **B.** 3

C. 7   **D.** 5

5.MD.C.3

36. How many centimeter cubes are needed to fill the rectangular prism?

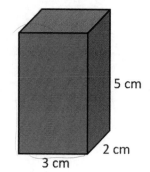

5 cm

2 cm

3 cm

_____ 30

5.MD.C.4

37. What is the volume of this solid?

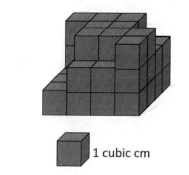

 1 cubic cm

_____ 38

5.MD.C.4

38. Reid is packaging this sculpture inside a box.

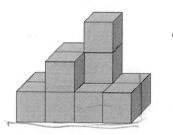

Turn it

The length of each cube is 3 inches. Which box should Reid use? Explain your reasoning.

...question 38. continued next page

prepaze

COMPREHENSIVE ASSESSMENTS

Box A	Box B	Box C
Length: 4 in	Length: 8 in	Length: 13 in
Width: 2 in	Width: 12 in	Width: 6 in
Height: 3 in	Height: 10 in	Height: 16 in

~~Box C~~ because right away

I can see that boxe's A and B have length's

~~smaller~~ than the sculpture   (Box B)

5.MD.C.5

39. Gabriel is packaging this sculpture inside a box.

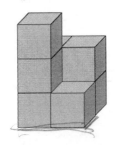

The length of each cube is 5 inches. Which box should Gabriel use? Explain your reasoning.

Box A	Box B
Length: 10 in	Length: 15 in
Width: 5 in	Width: 10 in
Height: 20 in	Height: 15 in

Box B because Box A's

width is too small

5.MD.C.5

prepaze

COMPREHENSIVE ASSESSMENTS

40. Place a point on the graph at the coordinates (3, 0).

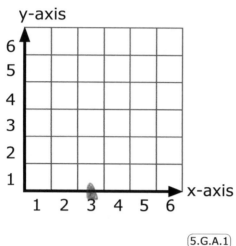

5.G.A.1

41. The coordinates of the pentagon are (4, 5).

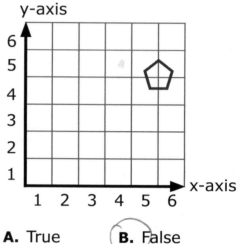

A. True   **B.** False

5.G.A.2

42. True or False: This quadrilateral is a trapezoid.

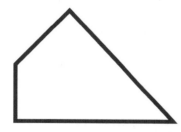

A. True

B. False

5.G.B.3

43. What name best describes this shape?

trapezoid

5.G.B.3

COMPREHENSIVE ASSESSMENTS

44. True or False: The name that best describes this shape is the square.

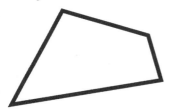

    A. True

    B. False

5.G.B.4

45. What name best describes this shape?

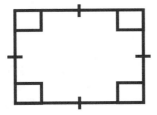

rectangle

5.G.B.4

ASSESSMENT ①

prepaze

ASSESSMENT ②

COMPREHENSIVE ASSESSMENTS

1. This expression equals 120.

$$(x + 9 \times 10)$$

What is the value for x?

A. 30 **B.** 55 **C.** 40 **D.** 20

(5.OA.A.1)

2. Fill in the blank with words. The value of Expression B is _____ the difference between 647 and 72.

Expression B: $(642 - 72) \div 3$

(5.OA.A.2)

3. The rule for the table is $y = 2x + 14$. What should the first number in the y column be?

x	3	5	7
y	?	24	28

A. 11 **B.** 20 **C.** 15 **D.** 10

(5.OA.B.3)

4. True or False: The rule of the table is $y = x + 11$.

x	5	7	9
y	17	19	21

A. True **B.** False

(5.OA.B.3)

prepaze

COMPREHENSIVE ASSESSMENTS

5. Write in the value of each digit in the number 89.365.

5: _____

9: _____

3: _____

8: _____

6: _____

5.NBT.A.1

6. The fifth grade class helped raise money to buy new schoolbooks. The following amounts were collected: 9 ten-dollar bills, 5 one-dollar bills, 3 dimes, and 4 pennies. The total amount of money that was raised in all was _____.

5.NBT.A.1

7. Solve: $71.32 \times 10^6 = $ _____

A. 71,320,000   **B.** 7,132,000   **C.** 713,200   **D.** 71,320

5.NBT.A.2

8. Solve: $2.33 \div 10^3 = $ _____

A. 233   **B.** 0.233   **C.** 0.0233   **D.** 0.00233

5.NBT.A.2

9. Write this number using words.

231.477

_____

_____

_____

5.NBT.A.3

COMPREHENSIVE ASSESSMENTS

10. Write the number in expanded form.

543.734

_____

5.NBT.A.3

11. Which number, when rounded to the nearest tenth, rounds up but when rounded to the nearest hundredth rounds down?

A. 4.395   **B.** 5.439   **C.** 5.939   **D.** 5.493

5.NBT.A.4

12. Joy wanted to buy 3 albums for $6.99, $7.99 and $5.99. She had a $20 gift card to spend. Which choice helps you illustrate whether she had enough money?

A. $6 + 7 + 5 = 18$ **B.** $20 - 6 - 7 = 7$

C. $7 + 8 + 6 = 21$ **D.** $6.5 + 7.5 + 5.5 = 19.5$

5.NBT.A.4

13. The school library has 62 shelves and each shelf holds 40 books. How many books are in the library?

A. 2,400 books   **B.** 2,480 books   **C.** 2,840 books   **D.** 3,200 books

5.NBT.B.5

14. Which two numbers can be combined to create a product of 625?

A. 5 and 120   **B.** 5 and 125   **C.** 25 and 100   **D.** 3 and 205

5.NBT.B.5

15. There are 8 fifth-grade classrooms going on a field trip. Each class has 24 students. If they are taking buses that hold 48 students, how many buses do they need to take?

A. 4   **B.** 40   **C.** 3   **D.** 5

5.NBT.B.6

prepaze

COMPREHENSIVE ASSESSMENTS

16. Noah divided 849 by 3. He said his quotient was 283 with 3 remaining. What was Noah's mistake?

  A. His divisor is incorrect.   **B.** His quotient is incorrect.
  C. His remainder is incorrect.   **D.** His quotient is incorrect.

5.NBT.B.6

17. Which expression has a value of 605.35?

  A. $605.35 + 423$ **B.** $630.75 - 24.5$ **C.** $3076 \div 5$ **D.** 121.07×5

5.NBT.B.7

18. Which expression equals 0.67?

  A. 10×6.7 **B.** $12.12 - 11.46$ **C.** $33.5 \div 5$ **D.** $8.56 - 7.89$

5.NBT.B.7

19. Alonzo has 2 white canvases. He paints $\frac{3}{8}$ of one of the white canvases red, and $\frac{2}{7}$ of the other white canvas blue. What fraction of the 2 canvases did the Alonzo leave white?

  A. $\frac{51}{56}$ **B.** $\frac{37}{56}$ **C.** $\frac{19}{56}$ **D.** $\frac{75}{56}$

5.NF.A.1

20. Brad went rock wall climbing. He got $\frac{6}{7}$ of the way up the rock wall and stopped. His left foot slipped and he fell $\frac{1}{4}$ of the way back down. How far up the rock wall is Brad now?

  A. $\frac{7}{28}$ of the way up the rock wall   **B.** $\frac{17}{28}$ of the way up the rock wall

  C. $\frac{5}{42}$ of the way up the rock wall   **D.** $\frac{17}{42}$ of the way up the rock wall

5.NF.A.1

COMPREHENSIVE ASSESSMENTS

21. Julie went to buy some candy for a gathering. She filled up the first bag with $\frac{8}{9}$ pounds of chocolate candies. She filled up a second bag with $\frac{3}{5}$ pounds of jelly beans. Which expression can be used to find the total number of pounds of candy Julie bought?

A. $\frac{8}{9} + \frac{3}{5}$ **B.** $\frac{8}{9} - \frac{3}{5}$ **C.** $\frac{3}{5} - \frac{8}{9}$ **D.** $\frac{8}{9} + \frac{8}{9}$

(5.NF.A.2)

22. Each circle represents 1 whole. Which fraction represents the combined shaded area?

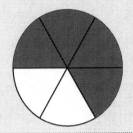 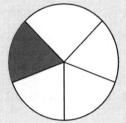

A. $\frac{6}{5}$ **B.** $\frac{5}{6}$

C. $\frac{13}{30}$ **D.** $\frac{26}{30}$

(5.NF.A.2)

23. Which expression shows $8 \div 14$ as a fraction?

A. $\frac{14}{8}$ **B.** $\frac{8}{14}$ **C.** $\frac{8}{22}$ **D.** $\frac{14}{22}$

(5.NF.B.3)

24. Which expression shows $15 \div 5$ as a fraction?

A. $\frac{5}{15}$ **B.** $\frac{5}{20}$ **C.** $\frac{15}{20}$ **D.** $\frac{15}{5}$

(5.NF.B.3)

25. True or False: $\frac{5}{6} \times \frac{3}{8} = \frac{15}{46}$

A. True   **B.** False

(5.NF.B.4)

26. True or False: $\frac{7}{9} \times \frac{5}{7} = \frac{35}{63}$

A. True   **B.** False

(5.NF.B.4)

COMPREHENSIVE ASSESSMENTS

27. Liam walked $5\frac{3}{8}$ miles around his neighborhood each day for one week. How many miles did Liam walk altogether after 7 days?

A. $37\frac{5}{8}$ **B.** $38\frac{5}{8}$ **C.** $39\frac{5}{8}$ **D.** $40\frac{5}{8}$

5.NF.B.5

28. Holly ordered $3\frac{1}{5}$ pounds of chocolate to make her famous dessert. If she only needs $\frac{2}{3}$ of what she originally ordered, how many pounds of chocolate will she use?

A. $2\frac{2}{15}$ **B.** $3\frac{2}{15}$ **C.** $2\frac{3}{15}$ **D.** $3\frac{3}{15}$

5.NF.B.5

29. Mary's gas tank held $20\frac{1}{10}$ gallons. If each gallon of gas costs $\$2.50$, how much will she spend to fill up her gas tank, if it is empty?

A. $\$50$ **B.** $\$50.25$ **C.** $\$50.50$ **D.** $\$50.75$

5.NF.B.6

30. Paul has a garden in which $\frac{3}{8}$ of the plants are flowers. Of the flowers, $\frac{1}{6}$ of the flowers are roses. What fraction of all the plants in Paul's garden are roses?

A. $\frac{1}{48}$ **B.** $\frac{2}{48}$ **C.** $\frac{3}{48}$ **D.** $\frac{4}{48}$

5.NF.B.6

31. What is the quotient of: $6 \div \frac{5}{7}$? _____

5.NF.B.7

COMPREHENSIVE ASSESSMENTS

32. This table shows the elevation of 4 mountains

Mountain	Kubi Gangri	Makalu	Antaleo	Distaghil Sar
Elevation (meters above sea level)	6,859	8,485	3,264	7,885

Which mountains have an elevation greater than 5 kilometers? Explain your reasoning.

_____

_____

_____

_____

5.MD.A.1

33. This line plot shows the weight of 12 oranges.

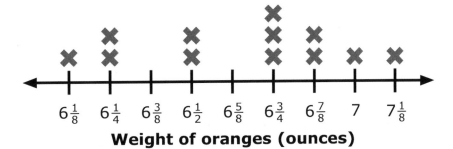

Weight of oranges (ounces)

How many oranges weigh more than $6\frac{4}{8}$ pounds?

_____

_____

_____

5.MD.B.2

prepaze

COMPREHENSIVE ASSESSMENTS

34. The units in the prism are one-third the size of the units in the small cube. How many of the small cubes will fit in the prism in the figure below?

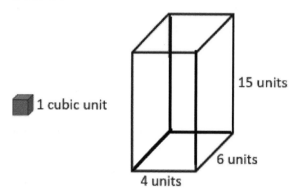

15 units

6 units

4 units

1 cubic unit

A. 120

B. 360

C. 150

D. 50

5.MD.C.3

35. Bo is filling this box with unit cubes.

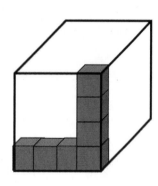

He uses 12 more cubes to fill the bottom layer. How many cubes will fit inside the box?

_____

5.MD.C.3

36. What is the volume, in cubic cm, of this solid?

1 cubic cm

_____

5.MD.C.4

COMPREHENSIVE ASSESSMENTS

37. This box is being filled with one centimeter cubes.

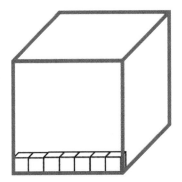

How could you determine the number of centimeter cubes needed to fill the base of this box?

_____

_____

_____

(5.MD.C.4)

38. Bo builds this rectangular prism using 2-inch cubes.

Bo removes 36 cubes from the center of the prism. What is the volume of this prism?

_____

_____

_____

(5.MD.C.5)

39. Which has a greater volume: a cube with a volume of 8 cubic feet, or a cube with edge lengths of 12 inches? Explain your reasoning.

_____

_____

_____

(5.MD.C.5)

prepaze

COMPREHENSIVE ASSESSMENTS

40. Place a point on the graph at the coordinates (5, 2).

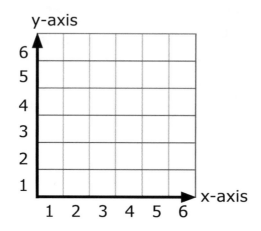

5.G.A.1

41. True or False: The coordinates of the triangle are (1, 5).

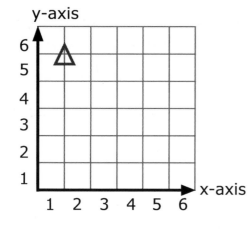

A. True   **B.** False

5.G.A.2

42. What name best describes this shape?

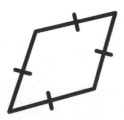

_____

5.G.B.3

COMPREHENSIVE ASSESSMENTS

43. What name best describes this shape?

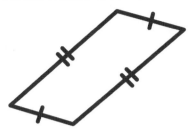

_____

(5.G.B.3)

44. What name best describes this shape?

_____

(5.G.B.4)

45. Based on the measures of the interior angles, what type of triangle is this?

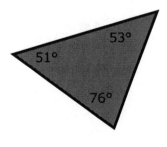

_____

(5.G.B.4)

prepaze

ANSWERS AND EXPLANATIONS

prepaze

OPERATIONS AND ALGEBRAIC THINKING: UNIT 1 - WRITE NUMERICAL EXPRESSIONS

1   Answer: Disagree.

Explanation: Answers must include a reasonable explanation such as, "I disagree. She must subtract $16-6$ is inside parentheses first." Correct order of operations requires the operation inside the parentheses to be performed first.

2   Answer: Multiply 9 and 5

Explanation: Answers must include a reasonable explanation such as, "Maria should multiply 9 and 5 first. According to order of operations we multiply first since there are no parentheses."

3   Answer: He is incorrect. Multiply first.

Explanation: Answers must include a reasonable explanation such as, "I would tell him that, to follow correct order of operations, and he should multiply first. He should multiply 72 by 2 and then add 9."

4   Answer: Add 5 and 11 or multiply 17 and 3.

Explanation: Answers must include a reasonable explanation such as, "Jacob should add 5 and 11 first because they are inside a parentheses." However, in this expression, multiplying 17 by 3 will not affect the answer.

5   Answer: C

Explanation: 3 times 1 equals 3 then 3 times 5 equals 15.

6   Answer: B

Explanation: 5 plus 20 is 25 divided by 5 is 5.

7   Answer: A

Explanation: Order of operations requires parentheses first. 9 plus 1 is 10. Then, 10 times 6 is 60, and 60 plus 15 is 75.

8   Answer: B

Explanation: 3 times 5 is 15, 15 plus 2 is 17.

9   Answer: C

Explanation: 8 minus 3 is 5, 5 times 15 is 75.

10   Answer: C

Explanation: If she subtracts 14 from 16 first, the expression will equal 50, so she should place the parentheses around $16-14$

11   Answer: D

Explanation: Each box has 2 rows of 6 crayons, so the expression must add 6 and 6 first and then multiply the answer by 11.

12   Answer: A

Explanation: To equal 18, the expression must include 2 x 9. The number 81 divided by 9 equals 9, so 4 + 5 must be performed first. Then 2 x 9 = 18.

13   Answer: B

Explanation: The left expression is simplified as follows:
$14+[24\div(8+4)]=14+[24\div12]=14+2=16$
The right expression is simplified as follows:
$6+(3\times11)-8=6+33-8=31$
The missing symbol is $<$.

14   Answer: D

Explanation: Solve for x by adding 15 to the right. Then subtract 29 minus 24 which equals 5; and then multiplying 5 times 30 which equals 150.

15   Answer: C

Explanation: Set the expression equal to 60. Subtract 27 minus 17 first, which is 10. Then, multiply 6 times 10, which is 60. Lastly, divided by 10. The value of c is 6.

16   Answer: B

Explanation: Add 4 plus 18 first, which equals 22. Then, multiply 22 times 2 resulting in 44. Last, subtract 100 minus 44 leaving 56.

17   Answer: B

Explanation: The left expression is simplified as follows:
$50-[2\times(4+4)]=50-[2\times8]=50-16=34$
The right expression is simplified as follows:

$17+(39÷3)+8=17+13+8=38$
Now, 34 is less than 38.

18 Answer: C
Explanation: Simplify the expression by performing the operations in the two parentheses first. The number 14 + 17 = 31, and 5 + 3 = 8. Next, 31 − 8 = 23. Last, 4 x 23 = 92.

19 Answer: B
Explanation: The left expression is simplified as follows:
$4×[9÷(2+1)]=4×[9÷3]=4×3=12$
The right expression is simplified as follows:
$60-[(9×3)+8]=60-[27+8]=60-35=25$
Now, 12 is less than 25.

20 Answer: D
Explanation: First multiply 4 and 10, which is 40; Adding 80 more to 40 will give the value of 120.

OPERATIONS AND ALGEBRAIC THINKING: UNIT 2 - INTERPRET NUMERICAL EXPRESSIONS

1 Answer: A quantity four times the sum of fifty-four and one hundred thirty-two
Explanation: Answers must include a reasonable explanation such as, "(54+132)×4 can be written as "four times the sum of 54 and 132."

2 Answer: Five times the sum of three and two.
Explanation: Answers must include a reasonable explanation such as, "The expression means five times the sum of three and two.

3 Answer: Disagree
Explanation: Answers must include a reasonable explanation such as, "I disagree, if the expression is correct, the words should be half as much, not twice as much. OR The expression should be (587−453)×2.

4 Answer: No
Explanation: Answers must include a reasonable explanation such as, "No, the expression would need a parenthesis around 675+93 to show three times a sum. As written, it shows 3 times 675 plus 93.

5 Answer: D
Explanation: The expression 12×(17+152) means 12 times the sum of 17 and 152. When an expression includes a number times a parentheses that includes a + or a −, it means the number times a sum or a difference.

6 Answer: D
Explanation: The expression 4 ×(5184 + 171) means 4 times more than the sum of 5184 and 171. When an expression includes a number times a parentheses that includes a + or a −, it means the number times a sum or a difference.

7 Answer: B
Explanation: The words require 17 and 4 to be added first, which means they are inside a set of parentheses. Then the sum is multiplied by 3.

8 Answer: A
Explanation: The expression 3×(15+4) means three times the sum of 15 and 4. When an expression includes a number times a parentheses that includes a + or a −, it means the number times a sum or a difference.

9 Answer: A
Explanation: Finding the quotient means to divide.

10 Answer: A
Explanation: The numbers 16 and 3 are multiplied first, then 7 is added and 1 is subtracted.

11 Answer: C
Explanation: The expression (3839 + 67) × 4 is 4 times the sum of 3839 +67.

When an expression includes a number times a parentheses that includes a + or a −, it means the number times a sum or a difference.

12 Answer: A

Explanation: $(100-15)\times3$ means the value 15 less than 100 is multiplied by 3.

13 Answer: 40÷(4+1)

Explanation: The expression $40\div(4+1)$ shows that 40 is divided by the sum of 4 and 1.

14 Answer: times

Explanation: $9\times(3+7)$ means nine times the sum of three and seven.

15 Answer: × or ·

Explanation: The word "product" means multiply two numbers which uses the symbol "×" or "·" to show the multiplication.

16 Answer: 11×6+7

Explanation: The expression $11\times6+7$ shows the product of 11 and 6 increased by 7. It can also be written as $11(6)+7$ or $11 \cdot 6+7$.

17 Answer: False

Explanation: To match the words, the expression needs to have parentheses. It should be $14\times(16+765)$.

18 Answer: True

Explanation: The expression $(2371-17)\div2$ can be written as the difference of 2371 and 17 then divided by 2.

19 Answer: False

Explanation: The expression with the parenthesis shows the product of 975 and 72, not the sum of 975 and 72.

20 Answer: True

Explanation: When an expression includes a number times a parentheses that includes a + or a −, it means the number times a sum or a difference.

OPERATIONS AND ALGEBRAIC THINKING: UNIT 3 - WRITE NUMERICAL EXPRESSIONS PATTERNS

1 Answer: (4, 8)

Explanation: Answers must include a reasonable explanation such as, "The next ordered pair is (4, 8). Start at (2, 4) and add 2 to x to get 4 and add 4 to y to get 8.

2 Answer: x + 6 and y −3

Explanation: Answers must include a reasonable explanation such as, "The rule for x is add 6 and the rule for y is subtract 3 because x increases by 6 and y decreases by 3.

3 Answer: (4, 9)

Explanation: Answers must include a reasonable explanation such as, "The second ordered pair is (4, 9). Start at (4, 9) and add 3 to 1 to get 4 for x and subtract 1 from 10 to get 9 for y."

4 Answer: x + 1 and y + 2

Explanation: Answers must include a reasonable explanation such as, "The rule for x is add 1 and the rule for y is add 2 because x increases by 1 and y increases by 2. This causes another rule that y is also always twice x."

5 Answer: B

Explanation: The first point is at (3, 2). The second pint is at (3 + 4, 2 + 2) which is at (7, 4).

6 Answer: B

Explanation: The rule for x is add 3. The rule for y is subtract 2. The missing pair is (7, 6).

7 Answer: C

Explanation: The rule for y is add 2, which gives a pattern 6, 8, 10. The missing number is 10.

8 Answer: C

Explanation: The first point is at (7, 7). The second point is at $(7-2, 7+1)$ which is at (5, 8).

9 Answer: A

Explanation: The numbers for y in the points are 5, 10, and 15, always increasing by 5 each point. Thus, the rule for y is add 5.

10 Answer: C

Explanation: The numbers for y in the table start with 15, then 13. This shows that the rule for y is subtract 2. Subtract 2 from 13 to get 11.

11 Answer: C

Explanation: The numbers for x in the points are 12, 9, and 6. This means rule for x is subtract 3.

12 Answer: D

Explanation: The rule for x is add 3, so to find the x in the point before another point, subtract 3 from the x-value. The rule for y is add 7, so to find the y in the point before another point, subtract 7 from the y-value. The ordered pair before (3, 7) is (0, 0).

13 Answer: B

Explanation: The rule is y is 8 less than x. $18 - 8 = 10$.

14 Answer: B

Explanation: The rule for x is add 2 to find the next x, and the rule for y is add 5 to find the next y. The next ordered pair is $(8 + 2, 15 + 5) = (10, 20)$.

15 Answer: D

Explanation: Each x-value is 9 less than each y-value.

16 Answer: A

Explanation: Using the rule, one option to find y is to write the equation $y = 3x$. Then, if $y = 6$, solve for x. The solution is 2.

17 Answer: False

Explanation: The rule of the table is $y = x+12$. Y is 12 more than x.

18 Answer: False

Explanation: The next ordered pair is at (5, 3) not at (3, 5). This pair has the rules reversed.

19 Answer: (14,1)

Explanation: To find the next point, start with (7, 7). The next point is found using the rule: $(7\times2, \frac{7}{7})$ which results in (14, 1).

20 Answer: True

Explanation: The table follows the pattern of x is always 5 less than y.

OPERATIONS AND ALGEBRAIC THINKING: CHAPTER REVIEW

1 Answer: I agree. Marcus is correct

Explanation: Answers must include a reasonable explanation such as, "I agree, the addition of 6 and 28 is inside the parentheses so it must be performed first."

2 Answer: Parentheses can represent grouping (as a grouping symbol) or the mathematical operation of multiplication

Explanation: Answers must include a reasonable explanation such as, "The parentheses tell which operation to perform first within the order of operation. Perform the operations inside the parentheses first and then perform the remaining operations in the expression."

3 Answer: 6 x (15 + 6)

Explanation: Answers must include a reasonable explanation such as, "Add 15 and 6 first to figure out how many writing utensils are on each table. Then, multiply that number by 6 to get the total number of writing utensils. The expression is $6 \times (15+6)$"

prepaze

ANSWERS and EXPLANATIONS

4 Answer: 85/5 + 29

Explanation: Answers must include a reasonable explanation such as, "To figure out how many pennies you have divide 85 by 5 and then add 29. The expression is 85 ÷ 5+29."

5 Answer: C

Explanation: Write an equation: $4(35-x)+4 = 72$. Subtract 4, leaving $4(35-x) =68$. Divide by 4, resulting in $35-x = 17$. Therefore $x = 18$.

6 Answer: A

Explanation: The left side simplifies as follows: $2[9(2 + 1)] = 2[9(3)] = 2(27) = 54$. The right side simplifies as follows: $50/[(2 \times 3) + 4] = 50/[6 + 4] = 50/10 = 5$.

7 Answer: C

Explanation: Write an equation: $5+(x\cdot10)=45$. Subtract 5 from both sides leavin $(x\cdot10)=40$. Divide both sides by 10. The solution is $x = 4$.

8 Answer: 4×(8+17)

Explanation: Answers must include a reasonable explanation such as, "4×(8+17). The sum of 8 and 17 means to add 8 and 17. The, multiply that sum by 4. Since the adding must be done first, the sum is in a parentheses."

9 Answer: The difference of six hundred fifty-four and fourteen divided by two.

Explanation: Answers must include a reasonable explanation such as, "(654 − 14) ÷ 2 is expressed using words as 'half of the difference between 654 and 14' OR 'the difference between 654 and 14 divided by 2' ."

10 Answer: 5×8−4

Explanation: Answers must include a reasonable explanation such as, "5×8−4 shows the product of 5 and 8 decreased by 4. The expression does not need parentheses because multiplication is performed first."

11 Answer: Yes

Explanation: Answers must include a reasonable explanation such as, "Yes. The difference means to subtract so subtract 135 from 5765 in parentheses. Then, to find half of that, divide by 2."

12 Answer: +

Explanation: Sum of two number means add them with a + sign.

13 Answer: 10×(15−9)

Explanation: The expression $10×(15−9)$ shows 10 times the difference of 15 and 9. When an expression includes a number times a parentheses that includes a + or a −, it means the number times a sum or a difference.

14 Answer: (3,5) (4,6) (5,7)

Explanation: The relationship between x and y, is $y = x + 2$. The next point is at (3, 3 + 2) or at (3, 5). Then, the next point is at (4, 4 + 2) or at (4, 6), and the third point is at (5, 5 + 2) or at (5, 7).

15 Answer: (3, 8) (4, 9) (5, 10)

Explanation: The first point is (2, 7) and the relationship between x and y is $y = 5 + x$. The next point is at (3, 3 + 5) or at (3, 8). Then, the next point is at (4, 4 + 5) or at (4, 9), and the third point is at (5, 5 +5) or at (5, 10).

16 Answer: y = x + 6

Explanation: Answers must include a reasonable explanation such as, "The rule is y=x+6, because the value of y is always 6 more than the value of x."

17 Answer: 31

Explanation: Answers must include a reasonable explanation such as, "The number 31 is missing from the pattern. Each value is 7 larger than the previous one".

18 Answer: B

Explanation: In the table, y is always 11 more than x, so 1 plus 11 is 12.

prepaze

19   Answer: B

Explanation: If the rule is $(x + 3, y + 5)$, then the sequence will be $(2, 4)$, $(5, 9)$, $(8, 14)$.

20   Answer: D

Explanation: If the y-value is 13 more than the x-value, then the x-value is 13 less than the y-value. Thus, 25 minus 13 is 12.

OPERATIONS AND ALGEBRAIC THINKING: EXTRA PRACTICE

1   Answer: B

Explanation: The terms being added and subtracted in the expression can be regrouped according to the associative property.

2   Answer: C

Explanation: The numbers inside the parentheses should be multiplied first and then added to 8.

3   Answer: 56

Explanation: A square has 4 equal sides, so the perimeter is $4[(3 + 4) + 7] = 56$. Another way is: The side length of the square is 14 units, so the perimeter is $4(14) = 56$ units.

4   Answer: 3 x [3 x (52÷2)]
        3(3 x 26)

Explanation: John walks 3 miles for 26 weeks out of the year over a period of 3 years. Change the sentence to an algebraic expression.

5   Answer: 177

Explanation: The expression could be simplified using these steps:

$25 + [120 + 4(15 - 7)]$

$= 25 + [120 + 4(8)]$

$= 25 + [120 + 32]$

$= 25 + (152)$

$= 177$

6   Answer: I disagree.

Explanation: The expressions do have the same value. The first expression is $[(32 - 19) - 15 - 2] = [13 - 15 - 2] = -4$. The second expression is $[32 - 19 - (15 - 2)] = [32 - 19 - 13] = 0$.

7   Answer: 42

Explanation: The expression could be simplified using these steps:

$38 + 56 \div (4 \times 2) - 3$

$= 38 + 56 \div (8) - 3$

$= 38 + 7 - 3$

$= 45 - 3$

$= 42$

8   Answer: D

Explanation: The missing value must be 12. Let w represent the unknown number. Expression A can be simplified to: $w(4 + 7)(8) = w(11)(9) = 88w$. Expression B can be simplified to $(4 + 7)(8)(4) = (11)(8)(4) = 88(4)$. Notice that both expressions contain a product of 88. Now, since Expression A is 3 times Expression B, $w = 3(4) = 12$.

9   Answer: A

Explanation: The numerical expression $9 - 4$ is written with words as "the difference of 9 and 4". However, 4 is being multiplied by $(10 + 7)$, which can be written as "the sum of 10 and 7". Therefore, the correct translation is "the difference of 9 and 4 times the sum of 10 and 7."

10   Answer: [4 x (54 + 6)]÷8 − 2

Explanation: When this verbal expression is translated into a numerical expression, the first 3 terms should be grouped together and since the words say "divided by the difference of", the last two numbers must also be grouped together.

11   Answer: (14 + 8) x (5 x 3)

Explanation: Since the words say "Add 14 and 8 and then … ". the sum of 14 and 8 are in parentheses so the addition is performed before the multiplication.

prepaze

12 Answer: [2 x (45÷9)] ÷ 5

Explanation: The verbal expression "twice" means the terms should be multiplied by 2. The verbal expression "the quotient of" means the terms should be divided.

13 Answer: No. Hunter is incorrect

Explanation: Hunter's representation of the number "one hundred three thousand, six hundred eight" should be 103,608.

14 Answer: Yes. Reynaldo is correct.

Explanation: The product of 18 and 19 can be expressed as 18 x 19. The product of 3 and 0 can be expressed as 3 x 0.

15 Answer: C

Explanation: The pattern shows adding 4 to the preceding x-value (6 + 4) and subtracting 3 from the preceding y-value (14 − 3).

16 Answer: A

Explanation: Since the value is the first ordered pair in the table, work backwards. Instead of subtracting 5, add 5 to find the x-value. Instead of adding 3, subtract 3 to find the y-value.

17 Answer: x-values: add 9 y-values: subtract 2

Explanation: Each x-value increases by 9, so the rule is add 9; each y-value decreases by 2, so the rule is subtract 2.

18 Answer: x-values: multiply by 3 y-values: divide by 5

Explanation: Each x-value is 3 times the previous value, so the rule is multiply by 3; each y-value is one-fifth of the previous y-value, so the rule is multiply by 5.

19 Answer: x-values: add 8 y-values: add 12

Explanation: Notice the scale on the axes. The ordered pairs shown on this graph are (8,8), (16,20), and (24,32).

20 Answer: x-values: add 9 y-values: add 3

Explanation: Notice the scale on the axes. The ordered pairs shown on this graph are (3,3), (12,6), and (21,9).

> **NUMBER & OPERATIONS IN BASE TEN: UNIT 1 - PLACE VALUE, ROUNDING AND COMPARING**

1 Answer: B

Explanation: First, in fraction form, remove 2 zeros from both numbers. Then divide 50 by 5. 5,000 ÷ 500 = 10

2 Answer: C

Explanation: Dividing by 10 moves the decimal one place to the left. 67.54 ÷ 10 = 6.754

3 Answer: C

Explanation: Dividing by 10 moves the decimal one place to the left. 9.32 ÷ 10 = 0.932

4 Answer: A

Explanation: Multiplying by 1/10 is equivalent to dividing by 10. Move the decimal one place to the left. 7,000 x (1/10) = 700

5 Answer: C

Explanation: Multiplying by 1/100 is equivalent to dividing by 100. Dividing by 100 moves the decimal one place to the left. 19.8 x (1/100) = 0.198

6 Answer: C

Explanation: Multiplying by 1/10 is equivalent to dividing by 10. Move the decimal one place to the left. 2.65 x (1/10) = 0.265

7 Answer: A

Explanation: 5.55 x 10 = 55.5. Multiplying by 10 moves the decimal one place to the right.

8 Answer: B
Explanation: 3.45 times 100 is 345. Multiplying by 100 moves the decimal two places to the right.

9 Answer: A
Explanation: $9 \div 10 = 0.9$ or $0.9 \times 10 = 9$

10 Answer: A
Explanation: $674 \div 100 = 6.74$ or $6.74 \times 100 = 674$.

11 Answer: 40
Explanation: The exponent of 10 is the same as the number of zeros for the place value. A 1 zero to the result because you are multiplying by 10 one time.

12 Answer: 7,000,000
Explanation: The exponent of 10 is the same as the number of zeros for the place value. Add six zeros because you are multiplying by 10 six times.

13 Answer: D
Explanation: Because the exponent of 10 is 4, add 4 zeros to 538 when multiplying: $538 \times 10,000 = 5,380,000$

14 Answer: A
Explanation: Because the exponent of 10 is 6, add 6 zeros to 44 when multiplying: $44 \times 1,000,000 = 44,000,000$

15 Answer: A
Explanation: Because the exponent of 10 is 0, do not add any zeros to 899: $899 \times 1 = 899$ Multiplying by 10^0 is the same as multiplying by 1.

16 Answer: D
Explanation: Because the exponent of 10 is 4, move the decimal 4 places to the right: $9.6 \times 10,000 = 96,000$

17 Answer: D
Explanation: The number 10^4 is 10,000, so $2 \times 10,000 = 20,000$.

18 Answer: A
Explanation: The decimal place was moved 3 places to the left. Thus, to retain the original value, multiply by 1,000: $660.43 \times 1,000 = 660,430$.

19 Answer: B
Explanation: The decimal place was moved 2 places to the left. Thus, to retain the original value, multiply by 100. The given expression ($82.6 \times 10,000$) is 826,000.

20 Answer: B
Explanation: The correct statement is $67.11 \div 10$ because $67.11 \div 100 = 0.6711$.

NUMBER & OPERATIONS IN BASE TEN: UNIT 2 - DECIMALS AND DECIMAL OPERATIONS

1 Answer: 315.162
Explanation: Three hundred fifteen is 315 and one hundred sixty-two thousandths is .162. The decimal place is where the word "and" is when the number is properly written with words.

2 Answer: 49.611
Explanation: Forty-nine is 49 and six hundred eleven thousandths is .611. The decimal place is where the word "and" is when the number is properly written with words.

3 Answer: 347.392
Explanation: $[3 \times 100 = 300]$ + $[4 \times 10 = 40]$ + $[7 \times 1 = 7]$ + $[3 \times (1/10) = 0.3]$ + $[9 \times (1/100) = 0.09]$ + $[2 \times (1/1,000) = 0.002]$. Then, $300 + 40 + 1 + 0.3 + 0.09 + 0.002 = 347.392$.

4 Answer: <
Explanation: The number $10.022 < 10.202$. Compare decimals beginning from the left, one digit at a time.

5 Answer: >
Explanation: The number $0.050 > 0.0050$. Compare decimals beginning from the left, one digit at a time.

6 Answer: =

Explanation: The two numbers are the same. Thus, 29.816 = 29.816.

7 Answer: >

Explanation: The left number is 100 + 50 + 2 + 0.6 + 0.3 + 0.002 = 152.632. Thus, 152.632 > 152.326.

8 Answer: C

Explanation: When rounding a number, review the place to the right of the digit the number is being rounded to. If the digit if 5 or more, round up, and if the digit is 4 or less, change all digits to the right of that place to 0.

9 Answer: B

Explanation: Although the directions say round to the tenths, because each of the numbers rounds up, the number eventually rounds up to the next whole number.

10 Answer: D

Explanation: The hundred-thousandth place is 5 or more, so round the ten-thousandth place from 3 up to 4.

11 Answer: A

Explanation: Since her answer has 4 decimal places, the number ends with the ten-thousandth place, so she was asked to round to the nearest ten-thousandths.

12 Answer: D

Explanation: The thousandths place is 5 or more, so round the hundredths place from 7 up to 8.

13 Answer: B

Explanation: Because the thousandths place is 5 or more, round the hundredths place up. However rounding 9, in the hundredths place, up automatically forces the tenths digit to be rounded up as well.

14 Answer: B

Explanation: To estimate a sum, round each number before adding. thus before performing 84.67+29.93, round 84.67 to 85 and 29.93 30. Then add 85 + 30.

15 Answer: C

Explanation: To calculate the change, subtract $29.75 from $40.00.

16 Answer: D

Explanation: To solve the equation, divide 6.4 by 0.8.

17 Answer: A

Explanation: First round 2.9 to 3 and multiply by 23. 23 times 3 is 69

18 Answer: A

Explanation: To find the factor, divide 34 by 4.25.

19 Answer: $6.55

Explanation: To find the sales tax, subtract $52.76 − $46.21.

20 Answer: 0.5

Explanation: To solve the equation, divide 4.9 by 9.

NUMBER & OPERATIONS IN BASE TEN: UNIT 3 - MULTIPLY AND DIVIDE

1 Answer: D

Explanation: When dividing, the problem is dividend ÷ divisor = quotient. In this problem, let the divisor be n. Now, substituting the values, you get 64 ÷ n = 2. What number times 2 gives you 64? The answer is 32.

2 Answer: C

Explanation: Dividing is dividend divided by divisor equals quotient. This problem is 72÷4, so the quotient is 18.

3 Answer: B

Explanation: When dividing, the problem is dividend divided by the divisor to equal quotient. In this problem, you know n ÷ 6=8. Consider what number divided by 6 is 8. The answer is 48.

4   Answer: A

Explanation: The best way to estimate the quotient is to round 6,629 to 6,600. Rounding to 7,000 will be very inaccurate and will not be a good estimate.

5   Answer: A

Explanation: Round 61 to 60 and then divide 60 ÷ 4, or divide first and then round the answer.

6   Answer: C

Explanation: Round 212 to 210 and then divide 210 ÷ 6, or divide first and then round the answer to the nearest whole number.

7   Answer: 96

Explanation: When dividing, the problem is dividend divided by the divisor to equal quotient. In this problem, 960 ÷ n = 10. You need to determine what number will go into 960, 10 times.

8   Answer: 32

Explanation: When dividing, the problem is dividend divided by the divisor to equal quotient. In this problem, 128 ÷ 4 = n. Divide 128 ÷ 4.

9   Answer: 280

Explanation: When dividing, the problem is dividend divided by the divisor to equal quotient. In this problem, n ÷ 20 = 14. You need to consider what number divided by 20 is 14. The answer is 280.

10   Answer: E

Explanation: Divide 37,000 ÷ 600. Then, round the answer.

11   Answer: B

Explanation: Multiply 5 × 500 and 4 × 400 and then add the answers.

12   Answer: D

Explanation: Multiply 12 × 8 × 4.

13   Answer: C

Explanation: Multiply 3 × 8 × 2.

14   Answer: A

Explanation: Add 320+15, then multiply that result by 8.

15   Answer: D

Explanation: Multiply 18 × 22.

16   Answer: C

Explanation: Multiplication is commutative, so multiply the three numbers, two at a time, in any order. For example: 128 × 4, and then multiply that result by 829.

17   Answer: B

Explanation: Multiply 50, 9, 2 in any order. 50 times 2 is 100; 100 times 9 is 900.

18   Answer: 16,128

Explanation: Multiply any two of the numbers and then multiply their product by the third number.

19   Answer: 54 hours

Explanation: Multiply 18 × 3; Include units.

20   Answer: 704 letters

Explanation: First find the total number of students by mutiplying 8 and 22. 8 × 22 = 176. Then multiply 176 with 4 to find a total number of letters. 176 × 4 = 704.

NUMBER & OPERATIONS IN BASE TEN: CHAPTER REVIEW

1   Answer: A

Explanation: The quotient 1,180.9 ÷ 10 = 118.09. Dividing by 10 moves the decimal point one unit to the left.

2   Answer: B

Explanation: Subtract 37.3 − 2.7 = 34.6. Then divide 34.6 ÷ 10 = 3.46.

3   Answer: A

Explanation: 29,029 x (1/10) = 2,902.9

4   Answer: $1,475.00

Explanation: Multiply by 100: $14.75 x 100 = $1,475.00

5   Answer: $1,205,000

Explanation: Multiply by 10,000: $120.50x 100 = $1,205,000.

6   Answer: 1,100

Explanation: First find the perimeter of the field Perimeter = 2(length + width) = 2(10,000+1,000) =22,000. Now, divide perimeter by 20 as there are fence posts every 20 feet. 22,000 ÷ 20 = 1,100

7   Answer: D

Explanation: Compare the decimals beginning with the first place to the right of the decimal point: 17.27 > 17.262 > 17.26 > 17.25

8   Answer: B

Explanation: There really is no need to compare the scores above 93. However, compare the decimal values beginning on the left next to the decimal point: 92.03 < 92.3 < 92.33 < 93.31

9   Answer: D

Explanation: 93.3 > 92.6

10   Answer: A

Explanation: First, 186 ÷ 8=23.25. This number must be rounded up to 24, so there is at least 1 counselor per 8 children.

11   Answer: B

Explanation: The hundredths digit is 7, which is odd, but when rounded the tenth digit is 4, which is even.

12   Answer: B

Explanation: 27+14=41, which will require 5 $10 bills to pay.

13   Answer: A

Explanation: Multiply 67 × 15.

14   Answer: A

Explanation: Multiply 6 × 12.

15   Answer: C

Explanation: Multiply 22 × 32.

16   Answer: C

Explanation: Divide 45 ÷ 15.

17   Answer: B

Explanation: The best way to solve this problem is to reduce both the dividend and the divisor by 10, which makes the problem 450 ÷ 5.

18   Answer: A

Explanation: When you divide 122 by 5, you get 24 with a remainder of 2.

19   Answer: $37,800 or $37,900

Explanation: Round 8.99 to 9 and round 4211 to 4200 and then multiply. Alternatively, multiply first and then round.

20   Answer: 7.65

Explanation: To find the answer, divide 45.9 ÷ 6.

NUMBER & OPERATIONS IN BASE TEN: EXTRA PRACTICE

1   Answer: 22.54

Explanation: Add 2.37, 1.8 and 18.37.

2   Answer: 2.16

Explanation: Subtract 8.7 − 6.54.

3   Answer: B

Explanation: On the first and second day, the miles is 455 + 365 = 820. Ten times 189 x 10 = 1,890, which is more than 820.

4   Answer: B

Explanation: The shipment contained 10 rolls of white fabric: 10 x 72.3 = 723 yards, and 4 rolls of black fabric: 4 x 112.3 = 449.2 yards. 449.2 x 10 = 4,492 > 723.

5   Answer: 6, 3, 9, 4

Explanation: 6 is in the ones place, 3 is in the tenths place, 9 is in the hundredths place, 4 is in the thousandths place.

6   Answer: 7.2

Explanation: Multiply the minutes by 100: 4.32 x 102 = 432. Then divide the product by 60 to convert the time to hours.

7 Answer: 160,000

Explanation: Multiply L x W x H = V: 40 x 40 x 10^2 = 160,000.

8 Answer: 24

Explanation: 7 x 6 = 42 hours a day; $10^3 \div 42$ = 23.81 days.

9 Answer: 0.011, 0.101, 0.110, 0.111, 0.112

Explanation: Compare decimals beginning with the first digit on the left. 0.011 < 0.101 < 0.110 < 0.111 < 0.112

10 Answer: 0.991, 0.919, 0.909, 0.099, 0.091

Explanation: Compare decimals beginning with the first digit after the decimal point. 0.991 > 0.919 > 0.909 > 0.099 > 0.091

11 Answer: C

Explanation: The rectangle has $\frac{4}{5}$ of its area shaded. Convert each fraction of shading to percent. The percent comparison is 80% > 75% > 50% > 25%

12 Answer: 14

Explanation: Divide: 671 ÷ 50 =13.42. All of the balls must be in a box, so round up to 14 boxes.

13 Answer: 4

Explanation: Add the prices: $25.99 + $35.95 = $61.94, which means she has to give the cashier 4 $20 bills, which is $80. Three $20 bills is $60.

14 Answer: 3.2377

Explanation: She should have rounded the last 6 up to 7 because of the 8 in the hundred thousandths place.

15 Answer: 144 presents

Explanation: Multiply 2 × 24 × 3.

16 Answer: No

Explanation: Multiply 20 × 10, to get how many pieces she has. She has 200 pieces. Now, multiply 15 × 15. She has 200 pieces, but she needs 225 pieces. She does not have enough candy.

17 Answer: 32

Explanation: Multiply 72 and 5, which is 360. To find the third factor, divide 11,520 by 360. The third factor is 32 because 5 × 72 × 32 = 11,520.

18 Answer: $10

Explanation: Multiply 35 × 6 and subtract that amount from 220.

19 Answer: 225

Explanation: To find how many apples were packed into the boxes, multiply: 18 × 12, then add 9.

20 Answer: His remainder was wrong.

Explanation: Dividing 68 by 6 gives 11 with a remainder of 2.

NUMBER & OPERATIONS - FRACTIONS: UNIT 1 - ADD AND SUBTRACT FRACTIONS

1 Answer: A

Explanation: To solve for x, cross multiply: 7x=42. x=6

2 Answer: C

Explanation: To solve for x, cross multiply: 4x=72. x=18

3 Answer: D

Explanation: To change $4\frac{5}{6}$ to an improper fraction, multiply 6 by 4 and add 5 for the numerator of the improper fraction: 6 x 4 + 5 = 29, $4\frac{5}{6} = \frac{29}{6}$

4 Answer: A

Explanation: To change $\frac{17}{4}$ to a mixed number, divide 17 by 4 to get the whole number portion. The remainder (1) is the numerator of the fraction portion: $\frac{17}{4} = 4\frac{1}{4}$

5   Answer: B

Explanation: To solve for x, subtract $\frac{6}{11}$ from both sides of the equation:

$\frac{74}{55} - \frac{6}{11} = \frac{74}{55} - \frac{30}{55} = \frac{44}{55} = \frac{4}{5}$

6   Answer: A

Explanation: Find the least common denominator, change the fractions, and combine them:

$\frac{5}{9} + \frac{3}{8} = \frac{40}{72} + \frac{27}{72} = \frac{67}{72}$

7   Answer: A

Explanation: Find the least common denominator, change the fractions, and combine them:

$\frac{3}{5} - \frac{4}{9} = \frac{27}{45} - \frac{20}{45} = \frac{7}{45}$

8   Answer: A

Explanation: The whole number portion of the mixed number is changed from 6 to 5 + 1:

$1\frac{1}{2} + 5 = 6\frac{1}{2}$

9   Answer: B

Explanation: In the expression, $3\frac{1}{2} - 2\frac{1}{4}$, just considering the whole numbers, $3 - 2 = 1$. So the expression cannot result in more than 2 and one fourth.

10   Answer: Determine common denominators for thirds and fourths.

Explanation: The expression $\frac{2}{3} + \frac{5}{4}$ can be rewritten with common denominators as $\frac{8}{12} + \frac{15}{12}$.
Or: when simplified, $\frac{8}{12} = \frac{2}{3}$ and $\frac{15}{12} = \frac{5}{4}$.

11   Answer: A

Explanation: If there are 14 people and each person will get an equal share, then each person gets to eat one part out of 14 parts, which is 1/14 of the lasagna.

12   Answer: A

Explanation: The problem states that 13 pieces of pizza were eaten. This means that 13/16 of the pizza was eaten, leaving 3/16 of the pizza left over.

13   Answer: D

Explanation: Subtract

$4\frac{1}{2} - 2\frac{2}{3} = \frac{4\times2+1}{2} - \frac{2\times3+1}{3} = \frac{9}{2} - \frac{8}{3} =$
$\frac{27}{6} - \frac{16}{6} = \frac{11}{6}$ or $1\frac{5}{6}$.

14   Answer: D

Explanation:
Add $\frac{6}{7} + \frac{3}{4} = \frac{24}{28} + \frac{21}{28} = \frac{45}{28}$ inches.

15   Answer: A

Explanation: Using common denominators:
$4\frac{1}{3}$ is equivalent to $4\frac{7}{21}$. $8\frac{2}{7}$ is equivalent to $8\frac{6}{21}$. The sum of $4\frac{7}{21}$ and $8\frac{6}{21}$ is $12\frac{13}{21}$.
Subtract $12\frac{13}{21}$ from 20; the result is $7\frac{8}{21}$.

16   Answer: A

Explanation: Find the common denominator of $\frac{1}{6}$ and $\frac{2}{5}$: $\frac{1}{6} = \frac{5}{30}$ and $\frac{2}{5} = \frac{12}{30}$ Altogether, $\frac{17}{30}$ of the candy bar is eaten. There is $\frac{13}{30}$ of the candy bar remaining.

17   Answer: B

Explanation: Find the common denominator of $\frac{1}{12}$ and $\frac{1}{15}$: $\frac{1}{12} = \frac{5}{60}$ and $\frac{1}{15} = \frac{4}{60}$ Altogether, they eat $\frac{9}{60}$ or $\frac{3}{20}$ of the tray of brownies.

18   Answer: B

Explanation: The fractions need to be converted to the common denominator. The mistake made here is that the numerators and denominators were added without finding the common denominators.

19 Answer: B

Explanation: Find the common denominator of $\frac{1}{4}$ and $\frac{1}{3}$: $\frac{1}{4} = \frac{3}{12}$ and $\frac{1}{3} = \frac{4}{12}$. So, $\frac{3}{12} + \frac{4}{12} = \frac{7}{12}$ of the class did work on math or reading and $\frac{5}{12}$ of the class did not work on math or reading.

20 Answer: B

Explanation: Find the common denominator (24); add the whole numbers (9 + 7) and the fraction (20/24 + 21/24)

NUMBER & OPERATIONS - FRACTIONS: UNIT 2 - FRACTION MULTIPLICATION

1 Answer: A

Explanation: The number 5 divided by 9 is written in fraction form as $5 \div 9 = \frac{5}{9}$.

2 Answer: B

Explanation: The number 5 divided by 9 is written in fraction form as $9 \div 4 = \frac{9}{4}$.

3 Answer: B

Explanation: The shaded area of the circle is $\frac{2}{5}$ of the entire circle. As a division problem, it is $\frac{2}{5} = 2 \div 5$.

4 Answer: D

Explanation: Seven parts out of eight parts of the octagon are shaded. As a division problem, $\frac{7}{8} = 7 \div 8$.

5 Answer: B

Explanation: When writing a fraction as a division problem, the problem becomes the numerator divided by the denominator. Thus, $\frac{21}{13} = 21 \div 13$.

6 Answer: D

Explanation: When multiplying fractions, multiply the numerators and multiply the denominators.
$8 \times \frac{1}{7} = \frac{8}{1} \times \frac{1}{7} = \frac{8}{7}$ or $1\frac{1}{7}$

7 Answer: A

Explanation: When multiplying fractions, multiply the numerators and multiply the denominators.
$\frac{4}{6} \times \frac{1}{5} = \frac{4 \times 1}{6 \times 5} = \frac{4}{30} = \frac{2}{15}$ when simplified.

8 Answer: C

Explanation: When multiplying fractions, multiply the numerators and multiply the denominators.
$\frac{6}{7} \times \frac{2}{9} = \frac{6 \times 2}{7 \times 9} = \frac{12}{63} = \frac{4}{21}$ when simplified.

9 Answer: B

Explanation: Multiply the numerators and multiply the denominators.
$\frac{9}{1} \times \frac{7}{8} = \frac{9 \times 7}{1 \times 8} = \frac{63}{8} = 7\frac{7}{8}$.
So, they need at least 8 cans.

10 Answer: C

Explanation: Multiply the numerators and multiply the denominators.
$\frac{6}{1} \times \frac{4}{9} = \frac{6 \times 4}{1 \times 9} = \frac{24}{9} = 2\frac{6}{9} = 2\frac{2}{3}$. So, they should order 3 buckets.

11 Answer: B

Explanation: Multiply
$9\frac{1}{4} \times \frac{1}{4} = \frac{37}{4} \times \frac{1}{4} = \frac{37}{16}$ which is less than $9\frac{1}{4}$ because $9\frac{1}{4} = \frac{37}{4} = \frac{148}{16}$.

12 Answer: B

Explanation: Comparing $1\frac{2}{3}$ and $1\frac{3}{10}$, compare the fraction parts: $\frac{2}{3}, \frac{3}{10}$. The fraction $\frac{2}{3}$ is greater than $\frac{3}{10}$.

13　Answer: A

Explanation: The shaded parts are the same size. In the first rectangle, $\frac{3}{4}$ represents 3 parts, and in the second rectangle, $\frac{1}{2}$ represents 2 parts.

14　Answer: less than

Explanation: Since the number 5 is multiplied by a fraction that is less than one, the value decreases. Alternatively: $5 \times \frac{2}{7} = \frac{10}{7}$ which is less than 5.

15　Answer: greater than

Explanation: Since the number 8 is multiplied by a fraction that is greater than one, the value increases. Alternatively: $8 \times \frac{6}{5} = \frac{48}{5}$ which is greater than 8.

16　Answer: C

Explanation: Multiply: $28 \times \frac{1}{4} = 7$

17　Answer: A

Explanation: Multiply $\frac{2}{3} \times \frac{1}{6} = \frac{2}{18} = \frac{1}{9}$

18　Answer: B

Explanation: Change the mixed number to an improper fraction and multiply. Cross cancel while multiplying: $\frac{14}{5} \times \frac{45}{1} = \frac{14}{1} \times \frac{9}{1} = 126$.

19　Answer: B

Explanation: Change the mixed number to an improper fraction and multiply. Cross cancel while multiplying: $\frac{30}{7} \times \frac{4}{9} = \frac{10}{7} \times \frac{4}{3} = \frac{40}{21}$ or $1\frac{19}{21}$ pounds.

20　Answer: C

Explanation: Change the mixed number to an improper fraction and multiply. Cross cancel while multiplying: $\frac{10}{3} \times \frac{12}{1} = \frac{10}{1} \times \frac{4}{1} = 40$ tubes

NUMBER & OPERATIONS - FRACTIONS: UNIT 3 - FRACTION DIVISION

1　Answer: $\frac{1}{8}$

Explanation: To simplify $\frac{3}{4} \div 6$, find the reciprocal of 6 and multiply $\frac{3}{4} \times \frac{1}{6}$, which is $\frac{1}{8}$.

2　Answer: $\frac{6}{35}$

Explanation: To simplify $\frac{6}{7} \div 5$, find the reciprocal of 5 and multiply $\frac{6}{7} \times \frac{1}{5}$, which is $\frac{6}{35}$.

3　Answer: $\frac{5}{18}$

Explanation: To simplify $\frac{5}{6} \div 3$, find the reciprocal of 3 and multiply $\frac{5}{6} \times \frac{1}{3}$, which is $\frac{5}{18}$.

4　Answer: $\frac{1}{18}$

Explanation: To simplify $\frac{4}{9} \div 8$, find the reciprocal of 8 and multiply $\frac{4}{9} \times \frac{1}{8}$, which is $\frac{1}{18}$.

5　Answer: $\frac{3}{16}$

Explanation: To simplify $\frac{3}{8} \div 2$, find the reciprocal of 2 and multiply $\frac{3}{8} \times \frac{1}{2}$, which is $\frac{3}{16}$.

6　Answer: $\frac{2}{63}$

Explanation: To simplify $\frac{2}{7} \div 9$, find the reciprocal of 9 and multiply $\frac{2}{7} \times \frac{1}{9}$, which is $\frac{2}{63}$.

7　Answer: $\frac{10}{3}$

Explanation: To simplify $2 \div \frac{3}{5}$, find the reciprocal of $\frac{3}{5}$ and multiply $2 \times \frac{5}{3}$ which is $\frac{10}{3}$.

8　Answer: $\frac{40}{3}$

Explanation: To simplify $8 \div \frac{3}{5}$, find the reciprocal of $\frac{3}{5}$ and multiply $8 \times \frac{5}{3}$ which is $\frac{40}{3}$.

9   Answer: B

Explanation: To simplify $\frac{1}{2} \div 3$, find the reciprocal of 3 and multiply $\frac{1}{2} \times \frac{1}{3}$ which is $\frac{1}{6}$.

10   Answer: C

Explanation: To simplify $\frac{1}{5} \div 6$, you must find the reciprocal of 6 and multiply $\frac{1}{5} \times \frac{1}{6}$ which is $\frac{1}{30}$.

11   Answer: B

Explanation: To simplify $\frac{2}{3} \div 5$, find the reciprocal of 5 and multiply $\frac{2}{3} \times \frac{1}{5}$ which is $\frac{2}{15}$.

12   Answer: B

Explanation: To simplify $\frac{3}{4} \div 4$, find the reciprocal of 4 and multiply $\frac{3}{4} \times \frac{1}{4}$ which is $\frac{3}{16}$.

13   Answer: D

Explanation: To simplify $2 \div \frac{1}{3}$, find the reciprocal of $\frac{1}{3}$ and multiply 2×3 which is 6.

14   Answer: D

Explanation: To simplify $8 \div \frac{1}{6}$, find the reciprocal of $\frac{1}{6}$ and multiply 8×6 which is 48.

15   Answer: A

Explanation: To simplify $\frac{1}{2} \div 6$, find the reciprocal of 6 and multiply $\frac{1}{2} \times \frac{1}{6}$ which is $\frac{1}{12}$.

16   Answer: A

Explanation: To simplify $6 \div \frac{1}{2}$, find the reciprocal of $\frac{1}{2}$ and multiply 6×2 which is 12.

17   Answer: B

Explanation: To simplify $\frac{1}{2} \div 4$, find the reciprocal of 4 and multiply $\frac{1}{2} \times \frac{1}{4}$ which is $\frac{1}{8}$ not $\frac{1}{6}$.

18   Answer: A

Explanation: To simplify $\frac{1}{4} \div 2$, find the reciprocal of 2 and multiply $\frac{1}{4} \times \frac{1}{2}$ which is $\frac{1}{8}$.

19   Answer: B

Explanation: To simplify $\frac{1}{3} \div 2$, find the reciprocal of 2 and multiply $\frac{1}{3} \times \frac{1}{2}$ which is $\frac{1}{6}$ not $\frac{1}{8}$.

20   Answer: A

Explanation: To simplify $3 \div \frac{1}{4}$, find the reciprocal of $\frac{1}{4}$ and multiply 3×4 which is 12.

NUMBER & OPERATIONS - FRACTIONS: CHAPTER REVIEW

1   Answer: D
Explanation: To solve for x, get x by itself on one side of the equation
$$x = \frac{2}{9} - \frac{1}{18} = \frac{4}{18} - \frac{1}{18} = \frac{3}{18} = \frac{1}{6}$$

2   Answer: D
Explanation: To solve for x, change the mixed numbers to improper fractions, with the same denominators, and get x by itself on one side of the equation.
$$x - \frac{4}{9} = 4\frac{12}{135}; \ x - \frac{22}{9} = \frac{552}{135}; \ x - \frac{330}{135} = \frac{552}{135}; \ x = \frac{330}{135} + \frac{552}{135} = \frac{882}{135} = 6\frac{8}{15}$$

3   Answer: C
Explanation: Change $3\frac{1}{5}$ to $\frac{16}{5}$ and $3\frac{4}{5}$ to $\frac{19}{5}$. Then subtract: $\frac{19}{5} - \frac{16}{5} = \frac{3}{5}$

4   Answer: A
Explanation: The student should change 8 to $\frac{48}{6}$ then $3\frac{1}{6}$ to $3 \times 6 + 1 = \frac{19}{6}$. Now subtract $\frac{48}{6} - \frac{19}{6} = \frac{29}{6}$ or $4\frac{5}{6}$.

prepaze

5   Answer: C

Explanation: Change the fractions so they have common denominators and then add them: $\frac{7}{9} + \frac{4}{7} = \frac{49}{63} + \frac{36}{63} = \frac{85}{63} = 1\frac{22}{63}$.

6   Answer: D

Explanation: Add the mixed numbers, without changing them to improper fractions: $7\frac{1}{8} + 5\frac{1}{4} = 7\frac{1}{8} + 5\frac{2}{8} = 12\frac{3}{8}$.

All answers are equivalent, one with a denominator of 32 and one as an improper fraction.

7   Answer: 4, 24 ÷ 6; $\frac{24}{6}$

Explanation: The question asks to divide 24 by 6: $24 \div 6 = \frac{24}{6} = 4$

8   Answer: 18 ÷ 10; $\frac{18}{10}$

Explanation: The question asks to divide 18 by 10: $18 \div 10 = \frac{18}{10}$ or $1\frac{8}{10}$

9   Answer: $\frac{8}{5}$ or $1\frac{3}{5}$

Explanation: The question asks to divide 8 by 5: $8 \div 5 = \frac{8}{5} = 1.6 = 1\frac{3}{5}$

10   Answer: B

Explanation: Multiply $\frac{1}{3} \times \frac{5}{6} = \frac{5}{18}$

11   Answer: A

Explanation: Multiply $12 \times 10\frac{1}{2} = \frac{12}{1} \times \frac{21}{2} = \frac{252}{2} = 126$.

12   Answer: A

Explanation:

$5 \times \frac{6}{7} = \frac{5}{1} \times \frac{6}{7} = \frac{5 \times 6}{1 \times 7} = \frac{30}{7}$.

13   Answer: less than

Explanation: Multiply $\frac{2}{5} \times \frac{1}{2} = \frac{1}{5}$ which is less than $\frac{2}{5}$.

14   Answer: Mr. Green has a larger driveway.

Explanation: Multiply the lengths and the

widths. The area of Mrs. Brown's driveway is $13\frac{1}{3} \times 6\frac{1}{3} = \frac{760}{3}$ square feet.

The area of Mr. Green's driveway is $7\frac{1}{3} \times 12\frac{1}{3} = \frac{814}{3}$ square feet.

15   Answer: B

Explanation: Multiply: $14 \times \frac{1}{7} = 2$.

16   Answer: D

Explanation: The figure shows 1 part out of 12 parts is planted with blueberries.

17   Answer: A

Explanation: Multiply: $\frac{1}{2} \times \frac{1}{2} = \frac{1}{4}$

18   Answer: B

Explanation: $(4 \times 2 + 1 = \frac{9}{2})$. $(3 \times 4 + 1 = \frac{13}{4})$. $\frac{9}{2} \times \frac{13}{4} = \frac{117}{8} = 14\frac{5}{8}$

19   Answer: $\frac{45}{4}$

Explanation: To divide $5 \div \frac{4}{9}$, change to multiplying by the reciprocal of $\frac{4}{9}$: $5 \times \frac{9}{4} = \frac{45}{4}$.

20   Answer: $\frac{63}{8}$

Explanation: To divide $7 \div \frac{8}{9}$, multiply by the reciprocal of $\frac{8}{9}$: $7 \times \frac{9}{8} = \frac{63}{8}$.

NUMBER & OPERATIONS – FRACTIONS: EXTRA PRACTICE

1   Answer: B

Explanation: Subtract: $9\frac{5}{6} - 2\frac{1}{2} = 7\frac{1}{3}$ not $7\frac{6}{12}$.

2   Answer: $\frac{6}{8}$, $\frac{9}{12}$, $\frac{12}{16}$

Explanation: To create an equivalent fraction, divide or multiply the numerator and denominator by the same number.

3   Answer: $\frac{8}{10}$, $\frac{12}{15}$, $\frac{16}{20}$

Explanation: To create an equivalent fraction, divide or multiply the numerator and denominator by the same number.

4   Answer: $\frac{3}{4}$

Explanation: $1 - \frac{1}{4} = \frac{3}{4}$

5   Answer: $\frac{4}{10}$ **or** $\frac{2}{5}$

Explanation: $\frac{9}{10} - \frac{5}{10} = \frac{4}{10} = \frac{2}{5}$

6   Answer: A

Explanation: $\frac{4}{9} + \frac{3}{8} = \frac{32}{72} + \frac{27}{72} = \frac{59}{72}$ of the class did work on math or reading assignment. So, $1 - \frac{59}{72} = \frac{13}{72}$ of the class did work on neither math nor reading.

7   Answer: $\frac{14}{3}$ **or** $4\frac{2}{3}$

Explanation: $14 \div 3 = \frac{14}{3} = 4\frac{2}{3}$

8   Answer: 25

Explanation: $125 \div 5 = \frac{125}{5} = 25$

9   Answer: $\frac{6}{22}$ **or** $\frac{3}{11}$

Explanation: Divide $6 \div 22 = \frac{6}{22} = \frac{3}{11}$

10   Answer: A

Explanation: Multiply: $\frac{4}{5} \times \frac{3}{4} = \frac{3}{5}$

11   Answer: B

Explanation: Find the area of the table by multiplying the length and width: $3\frac{1}{4} \times 2\frac{3}{5} = \frac{13}{4} \times \frac{13}{5} = \frac{169}{20} = 8\frac{9}{20}$ not $8\frac{6}{20}$.

12   Answer: A

Explanation: Find the area of the canvas: $9\frac{1}{8} \times 6\frac{2}{3} = \frac{73}{8} \times \frac{20}{3} = \frac{1460}{24} = 60\frac{5}{6}$.

13   Answer: C

Explanation: $4\frac{2}{7} < 4\frac{3}{7}$

14   Answer: C

Explanation: x is located 4 units out of 7 units after 3 meaning $x = \frac{4}{7}$.

15   Answer: D

Explanation: Multiply: $4\frac{2}{5} \times 10\frac{7}{8} = 47\frac{17}{20}$ which is slightly less than 48.

16   Answer: B

Explanation: Multiply $6\frac{1}{4} \times 6\frac{1}{4} = 39\frac{1}{6}$ not 25.

17   Answer: B

Explanation: Multiply: $20 \times \frac{1}{12} = \frac{20}{12} = 1\frac{2}{3}$ which is less than 2.

18   Answer: B

Explanation: Multiply: $3\frac{1}{6} \times 4 = 12\frac{2}{3}$.

19   Answer: A

Explanation: To find the answer, divide $12 \div \frac{1}{3}$. Change the problem to 12 times the reciprocal of $\frac{1}{3}$: $12 \times 3 = 36$.

20   Answer: C

Explanation: To find the answer, divide $10 \div \frac{5}{7}$. Multiply by the reciprocal of $\frac{5}{7}$: $10 \times \frac{7}{5} = 14$.

MEASUREMENT & DATA:
UNIT 1 - PROBLEM SOLVING - CONVERSION OF MEASUREMENTS

1   Answer: C

Explanation: The combined length is 13.93 cm. To convert cm to meters, divide by 100.

2   Answer: B

Explanation: Add 8 inches to 5 feet 5 inches is 5 feet 13 inches, or 6 feet 1 inch.

3   Answer: A

Explanation: Subtract the length of the eraser 0.65 cm from all pencils given in the table. Then multiply the resultant length by 10 to convert the cm to mm.

ANSWERS and EXPLANATIONS

4   Answer: D

Explanation: The combined length is 53.7 cm. To convert cm to meters, divide by 100.

5   Answer: B

Explanation: Subtracting 10 inches from 4 ft 9 inches resulting in 3 ft 11 inches.

6   Answer: C

Explanation: There are 12 inches in 1 foot. Mario's bat is 2 ft. 7 inches. Lulu's bat is 2 ft 5 in.

7   Answer: A

Explanation: $\frac{3}{4}$ of a foot is 9 inches. Oscar is 9 inches taller than Micah.

8   Answer: B

Explanation: There are 1,000 grams in 1 kilogram. The 4 books have a mass of 6,780 grams.

9   Answer: C

Explanation: There are 1,000 grams in 1 kilogram. The 3 books have a mass of 4,350 grams.

10   Answer: B

Explanation: There are 12 inches in 1 foot. Convert all mixed fractions to improper fractions. The total are that needs to be covered is: $12x \frac{85}{6} \times 12x \frac{55}{3}$.

Divide the total area to be covered with the area of each sheet to find how many sheets are needed.

$$\frac{12x \frac{85}{6} \times 12x \frac{55}{3}}{\frac{17}{2}x\ 11}$$

$12x \frac{85}{6} \times 12x \frac{55}{3} x \frac{2}{17} x \frac{1}{11} = 400.$

(Hint: Simplify before multiplying the numbers.)

11   Answer: D

Explanation: There are 12 inches in 1 foot. Convert all mixed fractions to improper

fractions. The total are that needs to be covered is: $12x \frac{25}{3} \times 12x \frac{25}{2}$

Divide the total area to be covered with the area of each sheet to find how many sheets are needed.

$$\frac{12x \frac{25}{3} \times 12x \frac{25}{2}}{4\ x\ 6}$$

$12x \frac{25}{3} \times 12x \frac{25}{2} x \frac{1}{4} x \frac{1}{6} = 625.$

(Hint: Simplify before multiplying the numbers.)

12   Answer: B

Explanation: There are 1,000 mL in 1 L. The empty space is $36 \times 1,000 \times \frac{1}{4}$ ml.

13   Answer: 3

Explanation: Convert 30 gallons to quarts by multiplying by 4. Then, divide by 40.

14   Answer: 60

Explanation: There are 2 cups in every pint. $30 \times 2 = 60$.

15   Answer: 16

Explanation: One gallons equals 128 ounces: $128/8=16$ glasses are needed.

16   Answer: 450

Explanation: 375 feet is equivalent to 4,500 inches. Divide 4500 by 30 to find the shoelaces produced in an hour. There are 150 shoelaces produced each hour, and 450 (150 x 3) shoelaces produced in 3 hours.

17   Answer: 198

Explanation: There are 12 inches in a foot. Dara needs 288 inches of ribbon, and currently has 90 inches (7.5 feet) of ribbon. $288-90=198$ are yet to be finished.

18   Answer: 0.8

Explanation: A 3200-meter race is equivalent to 3.2 kilometers. If each person runs the same distance, the distance run can be determined by dividing 3.2 and 4.

19   Answer: Answers may vary
Explanation: There are 16 ounces in

1 pound. Add the number of pounds and multiply by 16: 5.97 x 16 = 95.52 ounces.

20 Answer: No.

Explanation: Edward is incorrect. There are 16 ounces in 1 pound. Add the number of pounds and multiply by 16: 5.52 x 16 = 88.32 ounces.

> ### MEASUREMENT & DATA:
> ### UNIT 2 - GRAPHS AND DATA INTERPRETATION

1 Answer: B

Explanation: The data point "$\frac{1}{2}$" appears 5 times in the data set.

2 Answer: C

Explanation: The data point "$\frac{1}{4}$" appears 6 times in the data set.

3 Answer: A

Explanation: There are 6 insects that are $\frac{1}{4}$-inch in length. Add $\frac{1}{4}$ six times, or multiply 6 and $\frac{1}{4}$.

4 Answer: D

Explanation: There are 4 insects that are $\frac{1}{2}$-inch in length. Add $\frac{1}{2}$ four times or multiply 4 and $\frac{1}{2}$.

5 Answer: C

Explanation: Subtract $15\frac{1}{4}$ from $17\frac{1}{4}$.

6 Answer: A

Explanation: Subtract $28\frac{7}{8}$ from $29\frac{3}{8}$.

7 Answer: B

Explanation: Most 5th grade students are between the ages of 9 and 11.

8 Answer: C

Explanation: There are 3 data points on the 10 ½ marking.

9 Answer: D

Explanation: There are 6 data points

between $9\frac{1}{2}$ and 11. The numbers $9\frac{1}{2}$ and 11 are not included.

10 Answer: A

Explanation: There are 9 values (numbers) in the data set.

11 Answer: C

Explanation: There are 13 values (numbers) in the data set.

12 Answer: A

Explanation: There are 13 data points in the line plot which are greater than 1 inch.

13 Answer: $\frac{5}{4}$ miles

Explanation: The distance $\frac{5}{4}$ miles appears the most in this data set (3 times). It will have 3 data points on the line plot.

14 Answer: $8\frac{7}{8}$ lbs

Explanation: The value $8\frac{7}{8}$ inches only appears once in the data set.

15 Answer: $21\frac{1}{2}$ inches

Explanation: The combined length of the leaves could be determined by multiplying $5\frac{3}{8}$ and 4, or adding $5\frac{3}{8}$ four times.

16 Answer: $1\frac{1}{2}$ inches

Explanation: The difference between the longest and shortest leaf can be determined by subtracting $4\frac{5}{8}$ and $6\frac{1}{8}$.

17 Answer: 3.5 degrees Fahrenheit

Explanation: The highest recorded temperature is 88.5 or $88\frac{1}{2}$ degrees. The lowest temperature is 85 degrees. The difference between the highest and lowest temperatures is $3\frac{1}{2}$ (or 3.5) degrees.

prepaze

18   **Answer:**

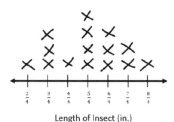

Length of Insect (in.)

Explanation: The line plot should display the data from the set with data points matching the frequency / number of times a value appears.

19   **Answer:**

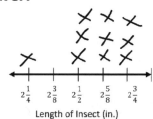

Length of Insect (in.)

Explanation: The line plot should display the data from the set with data points matching the frequency / number of times a value appears.

20   **Answer: There are 12 values or data points on this line plot. The difference between the highest and lowest temperatures is 4 degrees. The temperature that occurred the most is 93.5 degrees Fahrenheit.**

Explanation: Students may describe the line plot by evaluating the number of data points and what the data points represent.

MEASUREMENT & DATA: UNIT 3 - VOLUME OF SOLID FIGURES

1   **Answer: B**
Explanation: The base of the box can be filled with 16 cubes. There are currently 12 cubes, so 4 more are needed. The second level of the box would need 15 cubes $(16 - 1)$ to be filled.

2   **Answer: C**
Explanation: The smaller rectangular prism has a volume of 24 cubes. Since the volume of both prisms is 56 cubic units, the volume of the second prism is (56-24) or 32 cubic units.

3   **Answer: D**
Explanation: The base / first level of the box can be filled with 15 cubic units. There are 3 levels in the box. The box can be filled with (15 x 3) or 45 cubic units in the box. He already filled the box with 7 cubes. So, he would need 45 -7 = 38 cubes more.

4   **Answer: C**
Explanation: Count the cubes. This figure is made of 9 cubes.

5   **Answer: D**
Explanation: The product of 2 x 3 x 2 is 12 units. This figure is made of 12 cubes.

6   **Answer: 630 cubic units**
Explanation: The height of the box is 10 units. The volume can be found by multiplying the length, width, and height.

7   **Answer: 440 cubic units**
Explanation: The bottom of the box has an area of 55 square units. The volume of the box can be determined by multiplying the area of the bottom (base), by the height of the box (8 units).

8   **Answer: A**
Explanation: By multiplying the 3 dimensions of this box (30 x 12 x 2), it can be determined that the volume is 720 cubic units.

9   **Answer: C**
Explanation: The volume can be determined by multiplying the number of cubes in the base of the box by the height of the box.

10   **Answer: B**
Explanation: The volume can be determined by multiplying the number of cubes in the base of the box by the height of the box.

11   Answer: B
Explanation: The base layer has 16 cubic units. The number of cubes in each layer above it would be 14, 12 and 10 cubes. The volume is (16 + 14 + 12 + 10) or 52 cubic inches.

12   Answer: C
Explanation: The base layer has 32 cubic units. The number of cubes in each layer above it would be 29, 26, and 23 cubes. The volume is (32 + 29 + 26 + 23) or 110 cubic inches.

13   Answer: B
Explanation: The total volume of the box is 380 cubic centimeters. To determine the number of cubes on the bottom layer, divide the volume by the height. Dividing 380 by 19 is 20. There are 20 cubes in the bottom of the box.

14   Answer: A
Explanation: The total volume of the box is 280 cubic centimeters. To determine the number of cubes on the bottom layer, divide the volume by the height. Dividing 280 by 10 is 28. There are 28 cubes in the bottom of the box.

15   Answer: B
Explanation: The box is being filled with ¼ inch cubes. The width of the box is 28 cubes (7 x 4), the length of the box is 12 cubes (3 x 4), and the height of the box is 32 cubes (8 x 4). The number of cubes that will fill the box is (28 x 12 x 32) or 10,752 cubes.

16   Answer: A
Explanation: There will be 4 cubes for every inch of the box. In the first layer, which is 6 inches wide and 2 inches long, there will be (6 x 4) and (2 x 4) cubes.

17   Answer: D
Explanation: The number of boxes to ship (128 boxes) is divided by the volume of one crate to determine how many crates are needed.

18   Answer: A
Explanation: The large box has a volume of 27 cubic feet (3 x 3 x 3). Each small box has a volume of 0.125 cubic feet (0.5 x 0.5 x 0.5) Dividing 27 by 0.125 gives the number of small boxes that fit in each large box (27 ÷ 0.125 = 216) The, 500 ÷ 216 = 2.315 large boxes. Round 2.315 up to 3. It will take 3 large boxes, but the last box will not be full.

19   Answer: C
Explanation: The volume of each prism: Prism A – 9 cubic inches, Prism B – 18 cubic inches, Prism C – 60 cubic inches, Prism D – 27 cubic inches.

20   Answer: A
Explanation: The volume of each prism: Prism A – 9 cubic inches, Prism B – 20 cubic inches, Prism C – 24 cubic inches, Prism D – 18 cubic inches.

MEASUREMENT & DATA: CHAPTER REVIEW

1   Answer: D
Explanation: There are 16 ounces in 1 pound, which means there are (16 x 5) or 80 ounces in 5 pounds. Divide 80 by 5.5 and divide 80 by 5.9. The two answers are 14.5 and 13.6. The closest choice is 14.

2   Answer: A
Explanation: There are 16 ounces in 1 pound, which means there are (16 x 10) or 160 ounces in 10 pounds. Divide 160 by 5.4 and divide 160 by 5.1. The two answers are 29.6 and 31.4. The closest choice is 30.

3   Answer: 51,040
Explanation: There are 29 miles between Dallas and Ft. Worth. One mile is 1,760 yards. Multiply 1,760 x 29 = 51,040.

4   Answer: 12.5
Explanation: There are 5,000 meters in 5 kilometers. 5000/400 is 12.5.

5 Answer: B

Explanation: There are no data points on $1\frac{1}{4}$ or $1\frac{3}{4}$ inches.

6 Answer: C

Explanation: The lowest temperature is 90 degrees and the highest temperature is 94 degrees.

7 Answer: 5

Explanation: Even though there are 7 values to include on the line plot, two of the values ($\frac{5}{8}$ and $1\frac{1}{2}$) repeat themselves.

8 Answer: 7

Explanation: $6\frac{4}{8}$ is equivalent to $6\frac{1}{2}$. There are 7 oranges over this weight.

9 Answer: A

Explanation: Find the number of cubes by multiplying 64 by 9.

10 Answer: D

Explanation: The volume (324 unit cubes) can be divided by 6 to determine the total number of unit cubes in each layer.

11 Answer: B

Explanation: Determine the number of cubes in each layer by dividing 52 by 4.

12 Answer: D

Explanation: Determine the number of cubes in each layer by dividing 36 by 9.

13 Answer: 20 cubic inches

Explanation: The original solid has a volume of 8 cubic inches – adding 12 cubes creates a new volume of 20 cubic inches.

14 Answer: 56 cubic centimeters

Explanation: The original solid has a volume of 24 cubic centimeters – adding 4 additional layers adds 32 cubic centimeters to the prism.

15 Answer: 28

Explanation: Divide the volume by the number of layers (10) to calculate the number of cubes in each layer.

16 Answer: 384

Explanation: Multiply the length, width, and height to determine the number of sugar cubes that can fit inside the box.

17 Answer: 480 cubic inches

Explanation: The three dimensions of the shaded prism are 5 in., 8 in., and 12 in. Multiply them.

18 Answer: 456 cubic inches

Explanation: The volume of the outer rectangular prism is 1,824 cubic inches. Divide this value by 4.

19 Answer: 288

Explanation: There are 12 inches in 1 foot. When we use smaller cubes, we need to first convert the length of the sides into the smaller cube unit. So, the sides of the box are 96 in and 24 in.

The volume of the box is :

$$= 24 \times 96 \times 18 = 41472.$$

20 Answer: 38

Explanation: Volume of the crate is $5 \times 5 \times 5$ feet. Volume of each small box is $2.5 \times 2.5 \times 2.5$ feet. So, crate can hold $2 \times 2 \times 2 = 8$ small boxes. To find the total number of the crates required, divide 300 by 8. $300/8 = 37.5$ crates which rounds up to 38.

MEASUREMENT & DATA: EXTRA PRACTICE

1 Answer: Avi and Haley can ride the bus.

Explanation: One mile is 5,280. Divide each student's distance from school by 5,280 to determine the number of miles they live from school.

2   Answer: Kubi Gangri, Makalu, and Distaghil Sar.

Explanation: 1 kilometer is 1,000 meters. Three of the mountains have an elevation greater than 5 kilometers or 5,000 meters.

3   Answer: Gan is correct. Ian is incorrect.

Explanation: 72 inches is 6 feet and 3 yards is 9 feet.

4   Answer: Jada is correct, Diego is incorrect.

Explanation: One minute is 60 seconds, and 1 hour is 60 minutes. Thus 6 minutes is 360 seconds (60 x 6 = 360). However, $\frac{1}{12}$ of an hour is 60 minutes divided by 12, which is 5 minutes.

5   Answer: B

Explanation: There are 7 data points in the line plot.

6   Answer: There were between 0 and 1 quarts of orange juice consumed. Most students had 1 quart of orange juice. No students had $\frac{2}{8}$ or $\frac{7}{8}$ of orange juice.

Explanation: Answers may vary. Students may observe the total number of data points and how it represents the number of students included in the data set, the greatest amount of juice consumed, the least amount of juice consumed, and the number of student who consume fractional amounts of juice.

7   Answer:

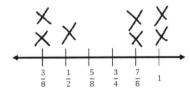

Amount of Paper (lb.)

Explanation: The line plot should display the data from the set with data points matching the frequency / number of times a value appears.

8   Answer: The difference in weight is 1 ounce.

Explanation: Subtract the least value from the greatest value.

9   Answer: B

Explanation: The box has 24 layers inside of it, since it took 8 layers to fill to $\frac{1}{3}$ of the capacity. To determine the additional number of unit cubes would fit inside the box, multiply 16 by 41.

10   Answer: D

Explanation: Two-thirds of the box is filled with 154 cubes, which means the box can be filled with 231 cubes. The base area of the box is 77 square units. Divide the total volume by the base area of the box to determine the height.

11   Answer: 280 cubic units

Explanation: The layer is the product of the length and width. Multiply the number of cubes in one layer by 10.

12   Answer: 140

Explanation: The volume of the outer prism is 560 cubic units (5 x 8 x 14). One-fourth of 560 is 140.

13   Answer: D

Explanation: Each smaller box can contain (3 x 3 x 3) or 27 candies. Each of the larger boxes can hold (4 x 10) or 40 candies. The total number of candies in all four boxes is (27 + 27 + 40 + 40) or 134 candies.

14   Answer: B

Explanation: The width of the box is half of 8 cm, which is 4 cm. The volume of each box is (8 x 7 x 4) or 224 cubic cm. There are 2 boxes, so they can hold 448 candies.

15   Answer: B

Explanation: Solid B contains 12 cubes, so its volume is 12 cubic units.

prepaze

ANSWERS and EXPLANATIONS

16   Answer: C

Explanation: The original prism has a total volume of 48 cubic units. If 8 cubes are removed, the new volume is 40 cubic units.

17   Answer: A

Explanation: The volume of the pool is 576 cubic feet (6 x 12 x 8). If the pool is ¾ full, then it contains 432 cubic feet of water.

18   Answer: C

Explanation: Find the volume of the pool by multiplying the length, width and depth (height). Then, multiply the volume by $\frac{3}{8}$.

19   Answer: The cube

Explanation: To calculate the volume of each prism, the dimensions should be multiplied. The value of 12 x 12 x 12 is greater than 6 x 4 x 2.

20   Answer: The cube with a volume of 1 foot is larger.

Explanation: The cube with edge lengths of 11 inches is less than a cube with edge lengths of 1 foot.

GEOMETRY:
UNIT 1 - GRAPHING AND COORDINATE PLANES

1   Answer: B

Explanation: To find the x-coordinate of a point, count the horizontal units from the origin to the point.

2   Answer: D

Explanation: To find the y-coordinate of a point, count the vertical units from the origin to the point. If the point is below the x-axis, the value is negative.

3   Answer: C

Explanation: To find the x-coordinate of a point, count the horizontal units from the origin to the point.

4   Answer: A

Explanation: To find the y-coordinate of a point, count the vertical units from the origin to the point. If the point is on the x-axis, the value is Zero.

5   Answer: A

Explanation: An ordered pair (x, y) describes the location of a point on the coordinate plane. The first number is called the x-coordinate, which is the number of horizontal units to the left (-) or right (+) of the origin, and the second number is called the y-coordinate, which is the number of vertical units up (+) or down (-) from the origin.

6   Answer: B

Explanation: An ordered pair (x, y) describes the location of a point on the coordinate plane. The first number is called the x-coordinate, which is the number of horizontal units to the left (-) or right (+) of the origin, and the second number is called the y-coordinate, which is the number of vertical units up (+) or down (-) from the origin.

7   Answer: A

Explanation: An ordered pair (x, y) describes the location of a point on the coordinate plane. The first number is called the x-coordinate, which is the number of horizontal units to the left (−) or right (+) of the origin, and the second number is called the y-coordinate, which is the number of vertical units up (+) or down (−) from the origin.

8   Answer: A

Explanation: An ordered pair (x, y) describes the location of a point on the coordinate plane. The first number is called the x-coordinate, which is the number of horizontal units to the left (−) or right (+) of the origin, and the second number is called the y-coordinate, which is the number of vertical units up (+) or down (−) from the origin.

9 Answer: B

Explanation: An ordered pair (x, y) describes the location of a point on the coordinate plane. The first number is called the x-coordinate, which is the number of horizontal units to the left $(-)$ or right $(+)$ of the origin, and the second number is called the y-coordinate, which is the number of vertical units up $(+)$ or down $(-)$ from the origin.

10 Answer: A

Explanation: An ordered pair (x, y) describes the location of a point on the coordinate plane. The first number is called the x-coordinate, which is the number of horizontal units to the left $(-)$ or right $(+)$ of the origin, and the second number is called the y-coordinate, which is the number of vertical units up $(+)$ or down $(-)$ from the origin.

11 Answer: $(1, -1)$

Explanation: An ordered pair (x, y) describes the location of a point on the coordinate plane. The first number is called the x-coordinate and the second number is called the y-coordinate. Point Q is 1 unit to the right of the origin and 1 unit downward from the origin.

12 Answer: $(-4, 1)$

Explanation: An ordered pair (x, y) describes the location of a point on the coordinate plane. The first number is called the x-coordinate and the second number is called the y-coordinate. Point S is 4 units to the left of the origin and 1 unit up from the origin.

13 Answer: $(-2, 5)$

Explanation: An ordered pair (x, y) describes the location of a point on the coordinate plane. The first number is called the x-coordinate and the second number is called the y-coordinate. Point P is 2 units to the left of the origin and 5 units up from the origin.

14 Answer: $(0, -4)$

Explanation: An ordered pair (x, y) describes the location of a point on the coordinate plane. The first number is called the x-coordinate and the second number is called the y-coordinate. Point R is neither left nor right of the origin and 4 units downward from the origin.

15 Answer: $(-5, -2)$

Explanation: An ordered pair (x, y) describes the location of a point on the coordinate plane. The first number is called the x-coordinate and the second number is called the y-coordinate. Point T is 5 units to the left of the origin and 2 units down from the origin.

16 Answer: $(-1, -5)$

Explanation: An ordered pair (x, y) describes the location of a point on the coordinate plane. The first number is called the x-coordinate and the second number is called the y-coordinate. Point U is 1 unit to the left of the origin and 5 units down from the origin.

17 Answer: $(1, 5)$

Explanation: An ordered pair (x, y) describes the location of a point on the coordinate plane. The first number is called the x-coordinate and the second number is called the y-coordinate. Point R is 1 unit to the right of the origin and 5 units up from the origin.

18 Answer: $(-1, -2)$

Explanation: An ordered pair (x, y) describes the location of a point on the coordinate plane. The first number is called the x-coordinate and the second number is called the y-coordinate. Point S is 1 unit to the left of the origin and 2 units down from the origin.

19 Answer: $(-6, 5)$

Explanation: An ordered pair (x, y) describes the location of a point on the coordinate plane. The first number is called the x-coordinate and the second number is called the y-coordinate. Point T is 6 units to the left of the origin and 5 units up from the origin.

20 Answer: (−4, −3)
Explanation: An ordered pair (x, y) describes the location of a point on the coordinate plane. The first number is called the x-coordinate and the second number is called the y-coordinate. Point U is 4 units to the left of the origin and 3 units down from the origin.

GEOMETRY:
UNIT 2 - PROBLEM SOLVING USING GRAPHING

1 Answer: B
Explanation: Starting from the origin on the x-axis, move 5 units to the right and up 4 units.

2 Answer: A
Explanation: Starting from the origin on the x-axis, move 4 units to the right and up 5 units.

3 Answer: C
Explanation: Starting from the origin on the x-axis, move 6 units to the right and up 1 unit.

4 Answer: D
Explanation: Find the picture of the restaurant and find the coordinates by moving down to the x-axis to find the x-coordinate and then across to the y-axis to find the y-coordinate.

5 Answer: B
Explanation: Find the picture of the car dealership and find the coordinates by moving down to the x-axis to find the x-coordinate and then across to the y-axis to find the y-coordinate.

6 Answer: A
Explanation: Find the picture of the radio tower and find the coordinates y moving down to the x-axis to find the x-coordinate and then across to the y-axis to find the y-coordinate.

7 Answer: D
Explanation: Find the picture of the hardware store and find the coordinates by moving down to the x-axis to find the x-coordinate and then across to the y-axis to find the y-coordinate.

8 Answer: D
Explanation: Starting from the origin, move 2 units to the right and 4 units up. The picture of the theater is at this point.

9 Answer: C
Explanation: Starting from the origin, move 3 units to the right and 1 units up. The picture of the harbor is at this point.

10 Answer: B
Explanation: Starting from the origin, move 2 units to the right and 6 units up. The picture of the dry cleaners is at this point.

11 Answer: (1,5)
Explanation: Moving left or right changes the x-value in the point. Starting at the point (2, 5) moving left one unit gives the point (2 − 1, 5) which is (1, 5).

12 Answer: (5,3)
Explanation: Moving left or right changes the x-value in the point. Starting at the point (2, 3) moving right 3 units gives the point (2 + 3, 3) which is (5, 3).

13 Answer: (4,4)
Explanation: Moving up or down changes the y-value in the point. Starting at the point (4, 3) moving up 1 unit gives the point (4, 3 + 1) which is (4, 4).

14 Answer: (5,1)
Explanation: Moving up or down changes the y-value in the point. Starting at the point (5, 3) moving down 2 units gives the point (5, 3 − 2) which is (5, 1).

15 Answer: (2,5)
Explanation: Moving up or down changes the y-value in the point. Starting at the point

(2, 4) moving up 1 unit gives the point (2, 4 + 1) which is (2, 5).

16 Answer: (1,6)

Explanation: Moving up or down changes the y-value in the point. Starting at the point (1, 4) moving up 2 units gives the point (1, 4 + 2) which is (1, 6).

17 Answer: (6,4)

Explanation: Moving up or down changes the y-value in the point. Starting at the point (6, 5) moving down 1 unit gives the point (6, 5 − 1) which is (6, 4).

18 Answer:

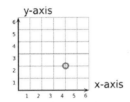

Explanation: Starting from the origin on the x-axis, move 4 units to the right and up 2 units.

19 Answer:

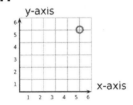

Explanation: Starting from the origin on the x-axis, move 5 units to the right and up 5 units.

20 Answer:

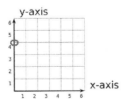

Explanation: Starting from the origin, do not move left or right, but move up 4 units.

1 Answer: D

Explanation: A quadrilateral is a shape with four sides. The shape appears to be a trapezoid,

2 Answer: B

Explanation: A right angle in a geometric figure is marked with a small square in the angle. The quadrilateral in the figure has four such markings.

3 Answer: C

Explanation: A square is a quadrilateral with four right angles and four equal sides.

4 Answer: C

Explanation: A rhombus is a quadrilateral straight sides where all sides have equal length. Also opposite sides are parallel and opposite angles are equal.

5 Answer: D

Explanation: A parallelogram has four sides with two pairs of congruent parallel sides.

6 Answer: B

Explanation: This is a trapezoid because two sides are marked parallel, and a trapezoid is a quadrilateral with exactly two parallel sides.

7 Answer: B

Explanation: A rhombus is a quadrilateral whose sides are all the same length. The figure shows a quadrilateral with two pairs of consecutive congruent sides, which is a kite.

8 Answer: A

Explanation: A quadrilateral is a shape with four sides.

9 Answer: B

Explanation: A rhombus is a quadrilateral whose sides are all the same length. The markings indicate the figure is a trapezoid.

10 Answer: A

Explanation: A parallelogram is a quadrilateral with two pairs of opposite parallel sides.

11 Answer: A

Explanation: A nonagon has 9 sides. The word nonagon could be written as 9-agon.

12 Answer: B

Explanation: A heptagon has 7 sides.

13 Answer: A

Explanation: Polygons are 2 dimensional closed shapes made of straight lines.

14 Answer: B

Explanation: An octagon has 8 sides.

15 Answer: A

Explanation: A regular polygon has straight lines and its angles and sides are the same.

16 Answer: Trapezoid

Explanation: A trapezoid is a quadrilateral with exactly one pair of parallel sides.

17 Answer: Rhombus

Explanation: A rhombus is a quadrilateral whose sides are all the same length.

18 Answer: Trapezoid

Explanation: A trapezoid is a quadrilateral with exactly one pair of parallel sides.

19 Answer: Trapezoid

Explanation: A trapezoid is a quadrilateral with exactly one pair of parallel sides.

20 Answer: Trapezoid

Explanation: A trapezoid is a quadrilateral with exactly one pair of parallel sides.

GEOMETRY: CHAPTER REVIEW

1 Answer: D

Explanation: An ordered pair (x, y) describes the location of a point on the coordinate plane. The x-coordinate is 5 units to the right of the origin. The y-coordinate is 4 units up from the x-axis.

2 Answer: C

Explanation: An ordered pair (x, y) describes the location of a point on the coordinate plane. The x-coordinate is 2 units to the left of the origin. The y-coordinate is 5 units up from the x-axis.

3 Answer:

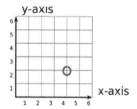

(4, 2)

Explanation: To find the x-location, from the origin move 4 units to the right. To find the y-location, move 2 units up from the x-axis.

4 Answer:

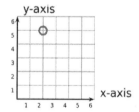

(2, 5)

Explanation: To find the x-location, from the origin move 2 units to the right. To find the y-location, move 5 units up from the x-axis.

5 Answer: A

Explanation: Find the picture of the party supply store and move down to the x-axis to find the x-coordinate and then across to the y-axis to find the y-coordinate.

6 Answer: D
Explanation: Find the picture of the art gallery and move down to the x-axis to find the x-coordinate and then across to the y-axis to find the y-coordinate.

7 Answer: D
Explanation: Find the picture of the magic shop and move down to the x-axis to find the xx-coordinate and then across to the y-axis to find the y-coordinate.

8 Answer:

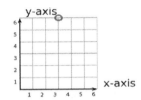

Explanation: To find the x-location, from the origin move 3 units to the right. To find the y-location, move 6 units up from the x-axis.

9 Answer: C
Explanation: A rectangle is a shape with four sides and four right angles.

10 Answer: A
Explanation: A square is a rhombus with four equal sides and four right angles.

11 Answer: D
Explanation: A quadrilateral is a polygon with four sides. The figure has four sides, but no other characteristics.

12 Answer: B
Explanation: A trapezoid is a shape with four sides and exactly two parallel sides.

13 Answer: B
Explanation: The markings in the figure show that only one pair of sides are parallel.

14 Answer: A
Explanation: A rectangle is a quadrilateral with four right angles. All of the angles are marked as right angles.

15 Answer: B
Explanation: A hexagon has 6 sides.

16 Answer: A
Explanation: A quadrilateral is a polygon with 4 sides.

17 Answer: B
Explanation: A regular polygon has its angles and sides are the same.

18 Answer: A
Explanation: A regular polygon has straight lines and its angles and sides are the same.

19 Answer: B
Explanation: The sides of a scalene triangle all have different lengths. The figure in the problem is an isosceles triangle.

20 Answer: A
Explanation: An isosceles triangle has 2 equal length sides.

GEOMETRY: EXTRA PRACTICE

1 Answer: (2, −3)
Explanation: Find the x-coordinate by moving horizontally, from the origin, to the right 2 units. Find the y-coordinate by moving vertically, from the x-axis, downward 3 units, to the point (2, −3).

2 Answer: (0, −4)
Explanation: Find the x-coordinate by not moving horizontally, from the origin, to the right or to the left. Find the y-coordinate by moving vertically, from the x-axis, downward 4 units, to the point (0, −4).

3 Answer: Point N
Explanation: Point N is located 3 units to

the right from the origin and 3 units upward from the origin. Thus, the coordinates of Point N are (3, 3).

4   Answer:

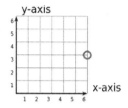

(6, 3)

Explanation: To locate the x-location, move horizontally, from the origin, 6 units. To locate the y-location, move vertically, from the x-axis, upward 3 units.

5   Answer: (4,0)

Explanation: Sue's house is located at (2, 4). Moving 2 blocks east is moving 2 units, horizontally to the right, from that point. Moving 4 blocks south is moving 4 units, vertically, downward from that point. The point becomes (2 + 2, 4 − 4) which is the point (4, 0).

6   Answer: (6,5)

Explanation: The star is at (3, 3); 3 units right and 2 units up the graph makes the location of the heart at (3 +3, 3 + 2) which is the point (6, 5).

7   Answer: (4,5)

Explanation: The diamond is at (6, 6); 2 units to the left and 1 unit down on the graph makes the location of the square at (6 − 2, 6 − 1) which is the point (4, 5).

8   Answer: (6, 6)

Explanation: The heart is at (2, 2). Starting at (2, 2), move 4 units to the right and 4 units down on the graph.

9   Answer: B

Explanation: A rhombus is a quadrilateral whose sides are all the same length.

10   Answer: B

Explanation: A square is a quadrilateral with four right angles and four equal length sides.

11   Answer: A

Explanation: A trapezoid is a quadrilateral with exactly one pair of parallel sides

12   Answer: B

Explanation: A trapezoid has exactly one pair of parallel sides. This polygon does not have parallel sides.

13   Answer: B

Explanation: A parallelogram has two pairs of parallel sides. This polygon does not have parallel sides.

14   Answer: A

Explanation: A trapezoid is a quadrilateral with exactly one pair of parallel sides.

15   Answer: A

Explanation: An isosceles triangle has 2 equal length sides.

16   Answer: B

Explanation: A right triangle has a 90° angle.

17   Answer: A

Explanation: A scalene triangle has 3 angles of different measures.

18   Answer: A

Explanation: An equilateral triangle has 3 equal sides.

19   Answer: B

Explanation: An obtuse triangle has one angle with a measure greater than 90°.

20   Answer: B

Explanation: A scalene triangle has 3 sides of different lengths and 3 angles with different measures.

1   Answer: D
Explanation: The expression 8 + 4 is in the innermost parentheses and should be simplified first.

2   Answer: 7
Explanation: The sum of the numbers 267 and 1,684 is multiplied by 7 so the answer will be 7 times the sum.

3   Answer: B
Explanation: Based on the pattern in the table, the next values are x = 8, y = 12, and then when x = 10, y will equal 15.

4   Answer: A
Explanation: The number 20 is ½ of 40, so when x = 20, y = 40.

5   Answer: 7, 2, 5, 1
Explanation: The number 7 is in the ones place, 2 is in the tenths place, 5 is in the hundredths place, 1 is in the thousandths place.

6   Answer: 0.02, 30, 0.007, 4, 0.8
Explanation: The number 2 is in the hundredths place, so its value is 2 x 0.01, 3 is in the tens place so its value is 3 x 10, 7 is in the thousandths place, so its value is 7 x 0.001 4 is in the ones place so its value is 4 x 1, and 8 is in the tenths place, so its value is 8 x 0.1.

7   Answer: B
Explanation: When multiplying a number by 10^2 , move the decimal place 2 places to the right because the multiplication is 7.82 x 100 = 782.

8   Answer: C
Explanation: 12.4 x 1,000 = 12,400.

9   Answer: fifty-eight and two hundred thirteen thousandths
Explanation: 58.213

10   Answer: six hundred seventy-nine and one hundred twenty-eight thousandths
Explanation: 679.128

11   Answer: A
Explanation: The hundredths place is a 4, so the number should be truncated to 2.3 not rounded up to 2.4.

12   Answer: D
Explanation: Divide 392 ÷ 48 which is 8.167. This number is rounded up to 9 so there are enough buses to carry all of the students safely.

13   Answer: C
Explanation: Multiply the pay per hour by the number of hours by the number of workers: 9 × 40 × 138.

14   Answer: D
Explanation: Multiply 15 × 1024.

15   Answer: D
Explanation: Add the number of bags of candy (5 + 10) and then divide the sum by 3.

16   Answer: D
Explanation: Divide 267 ÷ 30 = 8 with a remainder of 27.

17   Answer: B
Explanation: Multiply 2.5 × 63.

18   Answer: C
Explanation: To estimate the total, round to 40 and multiply by 12.

19   Answer: D
Explanation: Find the lowest common denominators and add the two fractions.
$\frac{3}{5} + \frac{1}{4} = \frac{12}{20} + \frac{5}{20} = \frac{17}{20}$

20   Answer: C
Explanation: Find the lowest common denominators and add the two fractions.
$\frac{7}{8} + \frac{1}{6} = \frac{42}{48} + \frac{8}{48} = \frac{50}{48}$

21   Answer: B

Explanation: Find the lowest common denominators and add the two fractions.

$$\frac{2}{5} + \frac{1}{3} = \frac{6}{15} + \frac{5}{15} = \frac{11}{15}$$

22 Answer: B

Explanation: The only possible choice is one that shows the difference $\frac{4}{5} - \frac{2}{3}$.

23 Answer: B

Explanation: The fraction represents part divided by whole. The rectangle is $\frac{9}{12}$ shaded: $\frac{9}{12}$ or $9 \div 12$

24 Answer: C

Explanation: When writing division as a fraction, divide the numerator (top number) by the denominator (bottom number): $4 \div 5 = \frac{4}{5}$.

25 Answer: A

Explanation: Change 4 to a fraction and then multiply the numerators and multiply the denominators.

$$4 \times \frac{2}{3} = \frac{4}{1} \times \frac{2}{3} = \frac{8}{3}$$

26 Answer: D

Explanation: Change 3 to a fraction and then multiply the numerators and multiply the denominators.

$$3 \times \frac{4}{5} = \frac{3}{1} \times \frac{4}{5} = \frac{12}{5}$$

27 Answer: D

Explanation: $\frac{3}{4} \times \frac{4}{5} = \frac{12}{20} = \frac{3}{5}$ meaning $\frac{3}{5}$ of the entire can of paint was used. All fractions shown in the answer choices are equivalent fractions for $\frac{3}{5}$.

28 Answer: C

Explanation: Multiply:
$1\frac{1}{3} \times 21 = \frac{4}{3} \times 21 = 4 \times 7 = 28$.

29 Answer: C

Explanation: Multiply:

$$2\frac{1}{8} \times 5\frac{2}{5} = \frac{17}{8} \times \frac{27}{5} = \frac{459}{40} = 11\frac{19}{40}$$

30 Answer: B

Explanation: Multiply 6.1 x 15 = $91.50.

31 Answer: 8

Explanation: To simplify $7 \div \frac{7}{8}$, multiply by the reciprocal of $\frac{7}{8}$: $7 \times \frac{8}{7}$ which is 8.

32 Answer: No Explanations may vary.

Explanation: There are 16 ounces in 1 pound. Estimating the weights, in pounds, 2 + 1 + 1 + 1 gives approximately 5 pounds, which means the weight is approximately 80 ounces.

33 Answer: The total weight is $52\frac{3}{4}$ ounces.

Explanation: Multiply each weight by the number of "Xs" above them in the line plot. Then add the products. The total weight of the oranges is $52\frac{3}{4}$ ounces.

34 Answer: B

Explanation: The area of the base is equivalent to 99 square units. There are 8 layers of cubes.

35 Answer: C

Explanation: In the context of the problem, the base of the prism is vertical. The area of the base is 80 square units. There are 7 vertical layers of cubes.

36 Answer: 30

Explanation: There are 6 cubes needed for each layer. There are 5 layers.

37 Answer: 38

Explanation: Use the figure to count the cubes on each layer. There are 16 cubes on the first layer, 13 cubes on the second layer, and 9 cubes on the third layer.

38 Answer: Box B

Explanation: Answers may vary. The dimensions of the sculpture are 12 inches long, 9 inches tall, and 6 inches wide. Box B has the closest dimensions to these without being too large. One box is too small, and one box is quite a bit too large.

39 Answer: Box B

Explanation: Answers may vary. The dimensions of the sculpture are 10 inches wide, 10 inches long, and 15 inches tall Box B matches these dimensions the closest.

40 Answer:

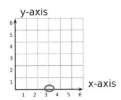

(0, 3)
Explanation: The point (3, 0) indicates that the point is 3 units to the right of the origin on x-axis.

41 Answer: B
Explanation: The x-coordinate is you the horizontal distance from the origin, and the y-coordinate is the vertical distance from the origin.

42 Answer: B
Explanation: A trapezoid is a quadrilateral with exactly one pair of parallel sides

43 Answer: Trapezoid
Explanation: A trapezoid is a quadrilateral with one exactly pair of parallel sides.

44 Answer: B
Explanation: A square has four 90° angles and 4 equal sides.

45 Answer: Rectangle
Explanation: A rectangle is a quadrilateral with two sets of congruent opposite sides and 4 right angles.

COMPREHENSIVE ASSESSMENTS
ASSESSMENT 2

1 Answer: A
Explanation: Write and solve the equation $(x+9\times10)=120$;
$x + 90 = 120$
$x = 120 - 90$
$x = 30$
The solution is $x = 30$.

2 Answer: less than or one-third
Explanation: The difference between the numbers will be divided which means it willbe less. The difference is divided by 3, which means it will be one-third the original value.

3 Answer: B
Explanation: Substitute 2 into the equation for x. Then, 2 times 3 is 6 and 6 plus 14 is 20.

4 Answer: B
Explanation: Every y-value is 12 more than the corresponding x-value. The rule of the table is y=x+12.

5 Answer: 0.005,9, 0.3, 80, 0.06
Explanation: The each digit in the number can be expanded as: (8 x 10 = 80), (9 x 1 = 9), (3 x 0.10 = 0.3), (6 x 0.01 = 0.06), and (5 x 0.01 = 0.005).

6 Answer: $95.34
Explanation: (9 x $10 = $90) + (5 x $1 = $5) + (3 x $0.10 = $0.30) + (4 x $0.01 =$ 0.04) + $95.34.

7 Answer: A
Explanation: Multiplying by 10^6 moves the decimal point 6 places to the right. Thus, 71.32 x 1,000,000 = 71,320,000.

8 Answer: D
Explanation: Dividing by 10^3 moves the decimal point places to the left. Thus, 2.33 ÷ 1,000 = 0.00233.

prepaze

9   Answer: two hundred thirty-one and four hundred seventy-seven thousandths

Explanation: The number 231 is written as two hundred thirty-one. Then, the decimal point is entered as "and". Lastly, the decimal 0.477 is written as four hundred seventy-seven thousandths.

10   Answer: 5 x 100 + 4 x 10 + 3 x 1 + 7 x (1/10) + 3 x (1/100) + 4 x (1/1,000)

Explanation: Expanded form is the sum of these digits: [5 x 100 = 500] + [4 x 10 = 40] + [3 x 1 = 3] + [7 x (1/10) = 0.7] + [x (1/100) = 0.03] + [4 x (1/1,000) = 0.004].

11   Answer: D

Explanation: The nine in the hundredths place rounds up but the 3 in the thousandths place rounds down and leaves the hundredths place the same.

12   Answer: C

Explanation: The only choice that is helpful is C, round each number to the nearest whole number and then compare the sum to 20.

13   Answer: B

Explanation: Multiply 62 × 40.

14   Answer: B

Explanation: The only numbers that gives a product of 625 are 5 × 125.

15   Answer: A

Explanation: Multiply 8 × 24 to get 192 students. Then, divide by 48 to get the number of buses needed.

16   Answer: C

Explanation: The number 849 divided by 3 gives 283 with no remainder.

17   Answer: D

Explanation: Multiplying 121.07 by 5 gives a product of 605.35.

18   Answer: D

Explanation: The difference between 8.5 and 7.89 is 0.67.

19   Answer: D

Explanation: Subtract the portion that was painted from the 2 Subtract the portion that was painted from the 2 canvases:
$2 - (\frac{3}{8} + \frac{2}{7})$. Find a common denominator, change all three terms, and then combine them.
$2 - \frac{3}{8} - \frac{2}{7}$
$\frac{112}{56} - \frac{21}{56} - \frac{16}{56} = \frac{75}{56}$

20   Answer: B

Explanation: Find a common denominator and subtract the two fractions
$\frac{6}{7} - \frac{1}{4} = \frac{24}{28} - \frac{7}{28} = \frac{17}{28}$

21   Answer: A

Explanation: To combine the fractions, find their sum: $\frac{8}{9} + \frac{3}{5}$.

22   Answer: D

Explanation: The shading in the first circle is $\frac{1}{5}$. The shading in the second circle is $\frac{4}{6}$. Combine: $\frac{1}{5} + \frac{4}{6}$, with a least common denominator of 30, (5 x 6 = 30). The sum is $\frac{26}{30}$.

23   Answer: B

Explanation: Division is expressed as dividend by divisor, and as a fraction, dividend over divisor: $8 \div 14 = \frac{8}{14}$.

24   Answer: D

Explanation: Division is expressed as dividend by divisor, and as a fraction, dividend over divisor: $15 \div 5 = \frac{15}{5}$.

25   Answer: B

Explanation: Multiply the numerators and multiply the denominators. Then simplify the answer by removing common factors:
(5 × 3)/(6 × 8) = 15/48 = 5/16

26 Answer: A

Explanation: The expression is correct, just not simplified. Multiply the numerators and multiply the denominators. Then simplify the answer by removing common factors:
$(7 \times 5)/(9 \times 7) = 35/63 = 5/9$

27 Answer: A

Explanation: Change the mixed number to an improper fraction or multiply the whole number and the fraction separately and then combine the products.
$5\frac{3}{8} \times 7 = \frac{43}{8} \times 7 = \frac{301}{8} = 37\frac{5}{8}$

28 Answer: A

Explanation: Change the mixed number to an improper fraction or multiply the whole number and the fraction separately and then combine the products.
$3\frac{1}{5} \times \frac{2}{3} = 2\frac{2}{15}$ means Holly will use $2\frac{2}{15}$ pounds of the chocolate she bought.

29 Answer: B

Explanation: Multiply the tank capacity by the price per gallon of gas: 20.1 x $2.50 = $50.25.

30 Answer: C

Explanation: Multiply the two fractions by multiplying the numerators and multiplying the denominators: $\frac{3}{8} \times \frac{1}{6} = \frac{3}{48}$.

31 Answer: $\frac{42}{5}$

Explanation: To divide $6 \div \frac{5}{7}$, find the reciprocal of $\frac{5}{7}$ and multiply $6 \times \frac{7}{5}$ which is $\frac{42}{5}$.

32 Answer: Kubi Gangri, Makalu, and Distaghil Sar.

Explanation: One kilometer is 1,000 meters. Three of the mountains have an elevation greater than 5,000 meters.

33 Answer: 7

Explanation: The weight 6 4/8 is equivalent to 6½. To weigh more than 6 ½, the orange is to the right on the line plot. There are 7 oranges to the right of 6 ½.

34 Answer: A

Explanation: The volume of the larger prism is 360 cubic units. One-third of 360 is 120.

35 Answer: 64

Explanation: The bottom layer already has 4 cubes in it. Twelve more makes the bottom 16 cubes. The prism has 4 layers. Thus, 4 x 16 = 64 cubes.

36 Answer: 30

Explanation: There are 16 cubes on the first layer, 10 cubes on the second layer, and 4 cubes on the third layer.

37 Answer: The box is in the shape of a cube, which means the length, width, and height are the same value.

Explanation: Assuming that the box is a cube, The box has a length, width, and height of 7 cubes, so the volume is 7 x 7 x 7 cubic centimeters. The number of cubes needed to fill the base will be 7 x 7 = 49 cubes.

38 Answer: 736 cubic inches

Explanation: The original prism is 8 x 4 x 4 cubes, which is 128 cubes. Since he removed 36 cubes, subtract 36 from 128. The prism now has 92 cubes. The volume of 1 cube is 8 cubic inches. Thus, 92 x 8 = 736.

39 Answer: The cube with a volume of 8 feet is larger.

Explanation: The cube with edge lengths of 12 inches is equivalent to a cube with edge lengths of 1 foot, which means it have a volume of 1 cubic foot.

40 Answer:

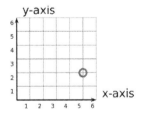

(5, 2)

Explanation: To find the x-coordinate, look for the first value on the horizontal axis and for the y-coordinate, look for the second value on the vertical axis. The point where the two values meet on the grid is the point.

41   Answer: A

Explanation: To find the x-coordinate, look for the first value on the horizontal axis and for the y-coordinate, look for the second value on the vertical axis. The point where the two values meet on the grid is the point.

42   Answer: Rhombus

Explanation: A rhombus is a quadrilateral whose sides are all the same length.

43   Answer: Parallelogram

Explanation: A parallelogram is a quadrilateral with two pairs of opposite congruent sides.

44   Answer: Quadrilateral

Explanation: A quadrilateral is a four-sided shape.

45   Answer: Acute

Explanation: An acute triangle has all angles less than 90°.

prepaze